God and Money

How to Make Money and Save Your Soul at the Same Time

Mike Mains

The author is indebted to the Brothers of Most Holy Family Monastery whose work was instrumental in educating him on many of the issues discussed in this book.

All Bible quotes in this book except for one come from the King James Bible. The King James Bible is not the most accurate translation of the Bible, but it is the most popular. It was chosen to make it easier for readers to verify the information presented here.

Author contact: mainsmike@yahoo.com

Contents

Preface

God, Money, and You

How does God feel about money?

Does God want you to be rich?

Does He want you to be poor?

Does God even care about how much money you have?

Is the Bible, as some have said, the world's greatest prosperity manual?

What does the Bible say about making money?

Is there a spiritual component to making money?

Why is the Bible quote, "The love of money is the root of all evil" frequently shortened to "money is the root of all evil"?

What does it mean to love money?

Why did so many saints take a vow of poverty?

Is there a science to making money?

If so, what is it?

You'll find the answers to these questions and a whole lot more inside the power-packed pages of this book.

Chapter One

Making Money is Easy

Making money is the easiest thing in the world. Don't let anyone tell you differently. What's not so easy is making money in ways that are pleasing to God. Because otherwise what's the point? You can make a billion dollars, engage in unlimited spending and unlimited sex, and then burn in hell for all eternity, but who wants that?

And yet that is exactly what almost everyone in the world is doing. They're not making billions of dollars, but many of them are making millions of dollars. Still more are making thousands of dollars. What they all have in common is they are making money in ways that are unpleasing to God, and then spending that money in ways that are even more unpleasing to God. As a result, almost everyone in the world today is on their way to hell.

Take usury, for example. Did you know that the Bible condemns usury? Yet if someone is invested in any type of interest-earning account, whether it's a savings account, a retirement account, or any type of account that's earning them interest, they are practicing and benefitting from usury, a sin that will likely send them straight to hell.

Even worse are those who charge interest, whether through credit cards, auto loans, student loans, home loans, etc. That includes every bank, auto dealership, collection agency, and college in the country. The people pushing those loans are all headed to hell.

But everyone is earning interest, you say. We all have bank accounts, 401(k) accounts, and treasury bonds. We're all doing it.

No, not everyone is doing it. *Almost* everyone is, but not everyone. And even if everyone was doing it, even if everyone in the entire world was earning interest, would that make it less of a sin?

In my book *How to Go to Heaven: Your Proven, Step-by-Step Plan to Achieve Eternal Salvation*, I go into great detail regarding the false belief that millions of people have that if everyone is doing something, it's no longer a sin.

Almost everyone on earth believes that if modern society condones and promotes a particular sin, then it is no longer a sin to engage in. They couldn't be more wrong. Sin is sin regardless of whether everyone on earth is committing it.

If you haven't already read that book, I urge you to do so. The majority of people reading this simply won't go to Heaven without the information contained in that book. Don't take my word for it. Read the book, verify its authenticity using the documentation and sources it contains, and see for yourself. In fact, a good rule of thumb is to never believe anything you've been taught or told, only what you have verified for yourself to be true.

It all boils down to this: The average person believes that if something is legal and morally acceptable by society's standards, then by natural extension it must also be morally acceptable to God and therefore not a sin to engage in.

Take the sin of homosexuality. The average person sees that homosexuality is not only legal, but morally acceptable and heavily promoted by society. As a result, they believe that homosexuality is not a sin to engage in.

The average person does this with a whole host of sins, including abortion, drug use, reading and watching pornography, sex outside of marriage, masturbation, birth control, immodest dress, usury, reading romance novels, buying and selling on Sundays, and more.

If you tell them that just because something is legal, that doesn't mean it's not a sin, you'll be met with a fluoride stare. The idea that something could be legal and heavily promoted on television, yet remain a sin, and not just any sin, but a sin that will send a person straight to hell, is simply incomprehensible to the average person. It's too much for their limited minds to grasp.

Those who push for more and more permissiveness know this and it's why they keep pushing. Their actions are less an attempt to undermine society as they are a coordinated attack on Christianity, with the intent to condemn as many souls to hell as they can.

We're at the point now in American society where large swaths of people believe it's perfectly acceptable to riot, loot, and shoplift. After all, they've had decades of media and academic indoctrination telling them that society owes them the very things they are stealing.

They can also see with their own eyes that if rioting, looting, and shoplifting were wrong in any way, then society would punish them for it. Instead society condones their behavior and encourages it. Thus, in their minds, it's acceptable behavior and not a sin to engage in.

Are they right?

If everyone in the world is engaged in the same sinful act, does that make it not a sin?

I think you know the answer.

Charging or collecting interest is not the only means in which people make money in ways that are unpleasing to God. How many people work on Sundays? That's also a sin—a direct violation of the Third Commandment.

How many people manufacture, sell, or dispense drugs? Doctors, nurses, and pharmacists all fall into that camp, along with school officials, teachers, and politicians who recommend and promote the use of drugs, including the forced "vaccination" of children.

There are also people who promote drugs via advertising, such as actors, writers, directors, film crews, etc. There are people who write and publish books filled with advice on what drugs to take, and websites doing the same thing, along with television networks that promote and advertise the use of drugs. And we haven't even touched on how many people are employed in the manufacture and shipping of drugs. Tally it up and you're looking at millions of people involved with the manufacture, sale, and dispensing of drugs.

But guess what? The Bible condemns drugs and calls them sorcery and witchcraft. Don't believe me? Pick up a Bible and see for yourself. (People disagree with me all the time on just about everything I say or write, but when I tell them to research the topic themselves and they take the time to do so, their jaws drop open. Remember, don't believe anything you've been taught or told, only what you have verified for yourself to be true.)

In this particular case, open your King James Bible to Revelations 18:23, and look at the last sentence. It reads, "For thy merchants were the great men of the earth, for by thy sorceries were all nations deceived." Then turn to a book called *Strong's Concordance.*

Strong's Concordance contains the Hebrew and Greek translations for every word in both the Old and New Testament. Take that book, open it to the Main Concordance, and find the word "sorceries." Scroll down the list under that word to Revelations 18:23 or Re 18:23. It will say, "by thy *s* were all nations deceived," followed by the number 5331. Turn to the back of the book where the Greek translations are, locate that same number 5331, and you'll see that it says, "pharmakeia from 5332; medication ("pharmacy"), i.e. magic, sorcery, witchcraft."

If you scroll down a couple of lines, you'll see that it also says, "Pharmakon; a druggist or poisoner, i.e. a magician, sorcerer." So there's your proof—the exact words written by St. John when he penned the last book of the Bible and condemned drugs as sorcery and witchcraft. Remember, too, that those words were communicated to St. John by an angel. Think about that. An angel, a representative of Heaven, told St. John in no uncertain terms that those who dispense drugs are poisoners, magicians, and sorcerers. Yet how many people today are dispensing drugs?

There's no ambiguity here. No ambiguity at all. The Bible has always taught that drugs are sorcery and that those who dispense them are sorcerers, witches, and poisoners. Weak-willed women and feminized men don't want to admit that, because they're cowards who hide from the truth, but there it is. Anyone involved with making, dispensing, promoting, or recommending drugs of any sort is guilty of the sin of sorcery, a sin that will send them straight to hell.

Are you beginning to see now how difficult it is to make money in ways that are pleasing to God? These two examples alone, usury and drugs, involve over 50% of the world's population and well over 90% of the population of the entire United States. And we've barely scratched the surface.

Now maybe you didn't know any of these things before, but you do now. And by the time you finish reading this book, you'll know a lot more—more than just about anyone on earth and certainly more than anyone you personally know. That I guarantee you.

What's more, every word you read here is documented in your favorite book—the Bible.

People think the Bible is a book about peace and love; a book advising them to be kind to everyone and not to judge others. They couldn't be more wrong. The Bible is both a history of the ancient world and a manual for living. It contains a strict set of rules for people to follow, and anyone who doesn't follow those rules is going to hell. I'm sorry, but that's the reality. It is not I telling you this, it's God.

Most people don't want to hear that. Maybe *you* don't want to hear it. But facts are facts. I'm obligated to tell you the truth, because I want you to go to Heaven. That's my whole purpose in writing this book. I'm not writing it for myself—I have all the money I need. I'm writing it for *you*— to help *you* go to Heaven.

Truth be told, I'd rather not be writing this book at all. I'd rather be writing fiction, which I enjoy, or not writing anything at all, because writing a book is hard work. It's much harder than most people think and I bet if you asked most people they would tell you that they think writing a book is hard.

When it comes to a book like this in which literally every statement is proven, verified, and backed up by evidence, it's even harder. I have to double, triple, and quadruple check everything. That's a lot of work.

Yet here I am, toiling late into the night and typing these words, because I want you to go to Heaven. And one of the necessary steps in order to do that is to make money in ways that are pleasing to God.

If you came to this book looking for a get-rich-quick scheme, well, you'll find that here, but you'll also find that making money in ways that are unpleasing to God will send you straight to hell. So while you *will* read valuable information here on the art of making money, most of it will be geared toward making money in ways that are pleasing to God. That's not as easy as making money the other way, but in the end you'll be happier.

A Fast and Easy Way to Get Rich

If you want to get rich as fast as is humanly possible, join your local Freemason lodge. Take their secret oaths and go through their initiations and once you're in, your Freemason brothers will open doors for you that seemed virtually impossible to open before. You'll rise to the top in whatever profession you choose. Nothing will prevent you from making massive amounts of money and attaining enormous success (so-called). What's more, you'll never go to jail for any crime no matter how crooked you are. To the outside world, it'll look as if you're leading the perfect life. Then you'll die and go straight to hell.

Is that what you want?

In an early edition of *How to Go to Heaven: Your Proven Step-by-Step Plan to Achieve Eternal Salvation*, I mentioned the secret to making hit movies. If that's what you want—if you want to be a famous movie producer or movie director, making millions of dollars and enjoying all the perks of that lifestyle, I can show you how to do that. The problem is if you follow that path, you're going to spend eternity burning in hell.

How can that be, you ask? I'll tell you how. When you work in the movie or television industry you're helping to put money into the pockets of some of the slimiest and most despicably evil people on earth, while simultaneously contributing to the moral rot of society. (I know. I've been there.)

And it doesn't matter what your role is. It doesn't matter if you're an actor, a grip, or whatever; you're part of that process. (You're also part of that process every time you pay money to see a movie or watch television.) In other words, if you work in the entertainment industry in any capacity, you're making money in a way that is very displeasing to God, which means you'll very likely be going to hell.

Is fame and fortune in this life worth burning in hell in the next? For many people it is, but what about you?

Let me state this as clearly as I can. If you're working for someone who hates Christ (and you are if you're working in the entertainment industry); if you're actively working to put money into their pockets and further their interests, yet you expect to somehow miraculously make it to Heaven in spite of all that, you're delusional. You're suffering from mental illness. I have a bridge in Baltimore I'd like to sell you.

St. John was very clear about this. He wrote: "Who is a liar but he that denieth that Jesus is the Christ? He is antichrist that denieth the Father and the Son." (1 John 2:22)

In other words, anyone who denies that Jesus is the Christ is going straight to hell. Yet when it comes to the entertainment industry, and that includes movies, television, music, and professional sports, you're not just dealing with people who deny that Jesus is the Christ, but with people who hate Jesus with a passion and spit in His face every chance they get. And the bigger their name, the more sick and depraved they are. Some of them are under blackmail. Some have literally sold their souls. And some relish the darkness they've embraced. I'm not joking about any of this. Yet there are hundreds of thousands of people, maybe even millions, who work in those industries and somehow think they will ultimately enjoy paradise in Heaven. How is that even remotely possible?

Why would God take a person like that into Heaven? Why would He allow someone into His kingdom that has spent their entire time here on earth actively working to enrich the lives of Christ-haters?

This is one of those points that no one ever thinks or talks about, yet it is vitally important for you to understand if you harbor any hope at all of going to Heaven.

For proof, open your Bible. "Be ye not unequally yoked together with unbelievers: for what fellowship hath righteousness with unrighteousness? And what communion hath light with darkness?" 2 Corinthians 6:14

But it won't affect me, you say? You believe you can work for those who deny Christ and not become corrupted yourself? If that's what you think, you're taking a huge risk.

"Can one go upon hot coals, and his feet not be burnt?" Proverbs 6:28

"It is impossible to be surrounded by flames and not to burn." Saint Cyprian

"It is impossible to maintain friendship with an evil person without becoming somewhat like him in evil." Saint Thomas Aquinas

What we're talking about is far worse than maintaining friendship with an evil person. It's working diligently to provide an evil person with financial gain.

You must also realize that those very people you're working for hold you in contempt. They despise you. Their hatred for you is so strong, they will go out of their way to tempt and corrupt you, without your even knowing it.

"He who leads a bad life cannot bear the sight of those who live well; and why? Because their life is a continual reproach to him." Saint Alphonsus Ligouri *Preparation for Death*

By the way, everything here also holds true for those who purchase products or services from evil people. Every time a person buys a book from a traditional publisher, or a movie ticket, or pays for cable television, or attends a professional sporting event, they're providing financial support to people who hate Christ, hate Christianity, and spit in the face of God. How can a person who provides such financial support hold even the slimmest hope of ever going to Heaven?

If that's you, then I beg you to reconsider your position and apply some common sense. And if you're working for people like that, people who hate Christ, you need to stop.

At this point, some of you are shaking your heads and saying, "This is taking things too far." But is it? We're talking about Heaven and hell, one or the other. There's no middle ground, other than purgatory, which eventually leads to Heaven. So you have to decide which side you want to be on. In that sense, we haven't gone far enough. And we're just getting started. Wait until you read the remaining chapters.

This issue is so vitally important that I'm going to repeat everything I've just said, and I'm going to do it in language so clear and so precise that even the most brain-addled individual can understand it.

The people who run and control the entertainment industry, which includes movies, television, music, sports, and traditional book publishing, are Christ deniers. They not only deny Christ, they hate Him with a passion. If you work for them on any level, or assist them financially *in any way*, such as buying their products or services, or, in the case of sports, watching and attending their games, you're contributing to their behavior. *You're denying Christ.*

What do you think is going to happen to you when you die? "But whosoever shall deny me before men, him will I also deny before my Father which is in Heaven." Matthew 10:33

You've got to pick a side here. You've got to take a stand. You're either with Jesus and His father in Heaven, or you're not. If you're not with God, you're with those who hate God.

It's amazing to me how people can behave so stupidly in regards to this issue. Even when it's spelled out clearly for them, as we've done here, they continue to damn their souls to hell.

Saint Anselm said, "If thou wouldst be certain of being in the number of the elect, strive to be one of the few, not of the many. And if thou wouldst be quite sure of thy salvation strive to be among the fewest of the few."

Being among the fewest of the few includes making money in ways that are pleasing to God. Who else besides me is ever going to tell you that?

17

Your Soul, Your Choice

So there you have it.

Are you ready to learn how to make money and save your soul at the same time?

Are you ready to take the plunge into making money in ways that are pleasing to God?

If so, prepare to be blown away by what you're about to read.

Your journey begins on the very next page.

Chapter Two

The Three Principles of Money

What is wealth? Most people would define wealth as money. But money is merely a medium of exchange and the paper money we currently use to buy things is essentially worthless as it's no longer backed by gold or silver. (Our monetary system, which became totally corrupt with the creation of the Federal Reserve in 1913, is the biggest scam in the world. Anyone who tells you otherwise, and that includes your teachers, parents, and professors, is a liar, a fool, or both.)

Even gold and silver can become worthless. When Hernan Cortes and his men overthrew the diabolically evil Aztec empire, they were showered with gifts of gold from neighboring Indian tribes. The Spaniards began shipping the gold back to their own country, but each time they unloaded a shipment in Spain, it caused the price of gold to go down, and the price for food and other essentials to go up.

Meanwhile, the English who found very little gold in the northeast territories of North America began shipping back to their native country fish, lumber, furs, and other essentials. In a very short time, England surpassed Spain as the world's most powerful country.

The gold that Spain was shipping back became essentially worthless, while the useful commodities that the English were shipping back contributed to the growth of their empire.

Money and Your Health

So what is wealth?

Some people say health is wealth. They make a stronger case than those who say that money is wealth. After all, what good is money if you're too sick to enjoy it? Yet people sacrifice their health for money every hour of every day.

There are lots of extremely rich people who have died unnecessarily from simple diseases like cancer and heart disease that they could have easily cured for little or no money, but they lacked the knowledge of how to do that.

Others suffer from crippling arthritis, another simple disease that can be easily cured for no money. But again, they lack the knowledge of how to do that.

All of which begs the question: can wealth be defined as knowledge? It can, and it makes more sense in the long run to value knowledge as wealth rather than money. Give me a choice and I'll take a wealth of knowledge over a wealth of money any day. The former can lead to the latter, but the latter can never lead to the former.

Then there are people who define wealth in terms of close relationships with friends and family members. That sounds great on the surface and it appears to make sense, but it really doesn't.

Your family and friends won't be with you on Judgment Day. You'll have to stand before God alone. That makes your relationships here on earth transitory to the extreme. The road to Heaven is a solitary journey. It's basically every man for himself.

Now if your family and friends are assisting you on that journey, they can be wonderful assets. If they're praying for you now and will pray for you after your death, then they could possibly help you get to Heaven. But the problem with that approach is it's putting your salvation in the hands of other people, rather than your own.

Finally, there are those who define wealth as spiritual wealth. I'm one of them. What good is all the money in the world, or the best of health, or all of the world's knowledge, or an abundance of wonderful relationships if you end up burning in hell for all eternity?

When you think of it in those terms, spiritual wealth is the only wealth that matters. Yet very few people are pursuing it. And the ones that are pursuing it are doing so through all sorts of pagan beliefs, false religions, and nonsense.

As you can see, there are different thoughts on just what wealth is. I've made my position clear. To me, spiritual wealth is the only type of wealth worth pursuing. Having said that, I know that many of you who are reading this book are looking specifically for tips and advice on making money. So let's talk about that first.

The First Principle of Money

One of life's basic laws is you can't get something from nothing. You can't get without giving. So in order to get, you first have to give. Giving before getting is God's way of living. First, you till the soil, then you plant the seed and water it (those actions constitute the giving part), and only after you have done those things do you reap the harvest (the getting part).

You can always give something, even if it's only a smile. In order to make money honestly and consistently in a way that's pleasing to God, you must provide something of value first. The something you give can be either a product or a service. That's the first principle of money. It's also immutable. When you give, you must receive something back that is of equal or better value.

At this point, you might be thinking of all the times you've seen people get without giving. It happens. We've all seen it, both in business and on the street. But those who take without giving first are committing a great sin; a sin they will eventually pay for either here on earth or in the afterlife.

I used to give motivational talks to people from low income neighborhoods and one of the first things I stressed was the concept of giving first in order to receive. Well, that part of my speech always went over like a lead balloon. I gave hundreds of those talks and almost no one who heard them was ever interested in giving before receiving. What they wanted to know was how much they could get without giving.

And get they did. Almost all of them were living on some form of government assistance—food stamps, welfare, EBT cards, free phones, you name it. And when it came time to vote, the ones who bothered to do so, voted only for whatever politician promised to give them more free stuff. That was their sole criteria.

The few people who paid attention to my talks and discovered ways in which they could give first before receiving did very well financially. While the majority who rejected that advice remained in poverty and are still in poverty today. The more they took without giving, the poorer they became.

Now obviously, if you're crippled or otherwise unable to work, then surviving on government aid is acceptable. After all, what else can you do? But anyone who is able to work but doesn't, and instead collects government aid for doing nothing at all is despicable. Such people are a cancer on society. They produce nothing of value, while taking from those who do. Today, tens of millions of able-bodied people living in the United States do just that. They sit at home, watching television and getting high, while living off the tax money that others pay.

There are also people who do work, but hold non-essential jobs as government workers and paper-pushers, contributing absolutely nothing to society. It seems like over half of the population in the United States is paid and rewarded for doing nothing at all.

When you give first in order to receive do it cheerfully, knowing that you are providing a product or service that benefits others. This is where a lot of people slip up. They're vaguely aware of the concept of giving before receiving, but they're not interested in benefiting others first.

The service or product they're offering is merely a cover—something of no real value, like the useless trinkets and beads the early American settlers offered to the Indians in exchange for gold and land, or the cheap plastic junk we see for sale in shops all over America.

In America today, almost every business in existence and the entirety of our country's government has forgotten the concept of giving before receiving. Their object isn't to make a good product which benefits the customer (giving before receiving), it's to make as much money as possible (taking without giving). Do you see the difference?

While it's true that most people are ignorant of the concept of giving before receiving (it's never taught in school), it's also true that most people are idiots, and along with their idiocy comes fear—fear of an unknown future.

That combination of fear and idiocy is the primary reason why nobody is concerned with fixing the problems of society. What they're concerned with is making enough money so the problems of society don't apply to them.

For men this is particularly appalling. Safety, comfort, and conformity are feminine values. When men embrace those values, when they sacrifice freedom for safety, and pursue money over truth, they're no longer men in the true sense, but merely facsimiles of real men. Yet that is exactly what most men are doing today. They've joined the ranks of the obedient, the brainless, and the walking dead.

The Second Principle of Money

The second principle of money is best described through the following quote.

> "Whatsoever thy hand findeth to do, do it with thy might; for there is no work, nor device, nor knowledge, nor wisdom in the grave, whither thou goest."—Ecclesiastes 9:10

What that means is to work hard at whatever you do; to do it with all thy might.

That doesn't mean moving at full speed twenty-four hours a day and wearing yourself out. It means showing up early, doing the best you can, and taking pride in what you're producing. It also means giving thanks to God for giving you an opportunity to turn your work into money.

A lot of people don't have that opportunity. Others do have it, but refuse to make the most of it. Rather than doing their work with all their might, they keep one eye on the clock and do their work as lazily as possible. With certain low-level, stress-inducing jobs, where the boss is a slave driver, out to exploit his employees for all he can, that type of slacker attitude is understandable. But most jobs aren't like that. If yours is, look for something else.

One of the keys to doing your work with all your might is finding your niche. Your niche is something in life that you can do better than anyone else on earth. If you're lucky or extremely talented, there are several things in life that you can do better than anyone else on earth. The trick is discovering them.

In addition to the thing that you can do better than anyone else on earth, there are things you can do where you might not be the best in the entire world, but where you are certainly in the top ten percent, or maybe even the top five percent. Make it your mission to find out what those things are and what your niche is.

Sometimes talents appear early in life and sometimes they appear late. And sometimes you have to give your talents up for God. I've known since a young age that I could write better than most people. Today, I don't consider myself the best in the world at it, but I do know that I'm in the top ten percent.

I didn't know that I had any acting talent until I was in my twenties. Now there I do consider myself among the best in the world. But when I discovered the truth about the movie business—it's a rotten, filthy business, run by rotten, filthy people—I had to give up acting and making movies for God.

You can see how that is a direct contradiction to what everyone else has ever told you about life, which is to "follow your dreams." But if I took that idiot advice, I'd be following my dreams straight into hell. That's because the movie business is run by Christ-hating devil worshippers. I'm not exaggerating when I say that. I mean it literally. In the same way that you and I worship God, they worship the devil.

They molest, rape, and murder children. They practice and promote rampant homosexuality. They constantly work to undermine Christianity and degrade society. They're the most evil and disgusting people imaginable. Yet the "follow your dreams" crowd would have me consorting with those very same people and helping to put money in their pockets.

"But it's your dream," they say, "your talent." True, but what good is talent and the fame that talent can generate if I end up burning in hell for all eternity?

When I tell people that I gave up acting and producing movies for God, they look at me like I'm crazy. Especially people I've worked with. But you see, they're all mired in the material world, where fame, money, and unlimited sex are simply too good to pass up. They think there must be more to the story than what I'm telling them. But no, there isn't. I gave up acting for God. I'm more concerned with where I'm going after I leave this world than with anything the world has to offer. "For the wisdom of this world is foolishness with God." 1 Corinthians 3:19

It's not just acting that I gave up for God. I'm one of the top-5 professional football handicappers in the world, but I had to give that up for God too. After the professional sports leagues all came out in support of the rioters and looters of BLM, after they all came out in support of homosexuality

27

and trannyism, after they all came out in support of the molestation and sexual mutilation of children, after they all came out in support of the phony pandemic and forced their players and coaches to take the jab that has now killed millions of people, and pushed their fans to do the same, what choice did I have? To continue any sort of relationship with professional sports would be akin to my endorsing all of those sins. On top of that, I would be providing financial support to those monsters. I would be making money in a way that is *very* unpleasing to God.

It's a decision that's costing me thousands of dollars, but it was either give up football for God or risk going to hell myself. The decision was painful but obvious.

That's enough about me and my talents. What are yours? What can you do better than most people and possibly better than anyone else on earth? Can you bake cupcakes better than anyone else on earth? Are you the world's greatest auto mechanic? What are your unique talents?

A black guy in New York who found himself crying at old movies, took that skill and became a professional crier. For a fee he'll attend a funeral and cry his eyes out. Other times he'll sit across the table, listen to someone's sob story, and respond with his own tears. Business is brisk.

A guy in Japan was constantly reprimanded by his bosses for "doing nothing." One boss told him, "Whether you're here or not, nothing ever changes." So he took the one thing he could do better than anyone else in the world—nothing—and turned it into money by renting himself out as "Do Nothing Rent-a-Man." Clients pay him to sit and share coffee in silence, to wave goodbye to them as they depart on a train, or to stand in the freezing cold as an audience for a street musician. His name is Shoji Morimoto and he's made close to a million dollars.

Like both of these men, there's something unique that you can do better than anyone else. If you don't know what that is, if you don't know what your talents are, relax. It will come to you if you look. Try different things. Ask yourself what you like doing more than anything else. That's usually a clue.

Doing your best—doing whatsoever thy hand findeth to do with all thy might—is the second principle when it comes to money. The third principle is productive enterprise.

The Third Principle of Money

In an ideal world, everyone would earn their livelihood through productive enterprise—producing products or services that other people need or want.

That's how life *used* to be and how honest men *used* to make their living. It's certainly a factor that contributed to the wellbeing and happiness of Christian Europe that flourished for hundreds of year.

Productive enterprise creates a win/win situation. Someone labors and receives compensation for producing a product or service of value, while someone else receives the benefit of the product or service they purchased. Everyone wins. In such a system, quality becomes the competitive and determining factor. Everything from clothes to furniture is made with quality and built to last.

People who engage in productive enterprise take pride in their work. For most people, men especially, this is an essential component of self-esteem. All men want to feel important and useful. Producing products of quality and good workmanship is a way for men to achieve that.

Work, when focused on productive enterprise, is a healthy and character-building endeavor. Men who own their own company or farm, or work for someone who does, benefit tremendously by such work, along with the customers who purchase their products.

Today, fewer and fewer people are producing products or services that other people need or want. Instead they are focused strictly on profit and how much money they can make. Nobody takes pride in their work, because society no longer judges men by the quality of what they do, it judges them only by how much money they make.

Quality has gone out the window, and that's why everything you buy today falls apart after six months, why it's all cheap, shoddy junk. It's why the price for everything you buy has gone up, while the size and packaging of those same products has gone down. It's why your landlord keeps raising your rent and why your energy bills grow higher and higher. Even worse, more people than ever today have abandoned productive enterprise entirely and instead focus on speculation.

Speculation is making money for money's sake. In speculation, nothing is produced or sold. It's using money to make money through stocks, bonds, interest, etc. Notice here how the first principal of money is completely ignored. Nothing is first being given in order to receive. (This is one of the reasons why usury is such a serious sin.)

In speculation, since nothing is produced, one party benefits (the party that makes money), while another party loses (the party that suffers loss in the exchange). Compare that to productive enterprise in which all parties benefit.

While speculation of this sort is legal throughout the world, it's condemned in the Bible. If you remember the story of Jesus fastening a whip out of cords and driving the money changers out of the temple, that was because they were charging interest—usury—on the people. It's the only instance in the Bible where Jesus displays outright physical hostility.

Knowing that, are you sure you want to engage in speculation and usury?

I'm not going to do it. I refuse to participate in usury in any shape, way, or form. Even with the money I keep in the bank. I have it in an interest-free checking account.

If God condemns usury and says it's wrong, then I don't want any part of it. I'm committed to living my life according to God's laws, not man's laws. And I'm certainly not interested in doing the same thing that everyone else in the world is doing. Remember: "For the wisdom of this world is foolishness with God." 1 Corinthians 3:19

Speculation is rampant in society today. And people do make money at it. But what good is that money going to do them when they die and go to hell?

Forget What Everyone Else has Ever Told You

Can you see now why the concept of "do what you love and the money will follow" is total trash?

That idea was big with the boomer generation and it has helped send countless souls to hell.

Doctors and nurses love poisoning people with fake vaccines.

Lawyers love lying in court.

Judges love perverting justice.

Sexual deviants love molesting and mutilating children and turning them into trannies.

Sick perverts love producing pornography.

Al Goldstein, a major producer of pornography was asked why he did it. He said, "The only reason why Jews are in pornography is that we think Christ sucks. Catholicism sucks. Pornography thus becomes a way of defiling Christian culture."

People like that litter the world. They're all following that old adage of do what you love and the money will follow.

A far better philosophy is to do what you like and are good at, but only if it's pleasing to God. If it's not pleasing to God, forget it.

Your Soul, Your Choice

My advice to you is to engage in the three principles of money: to give before getting, to do your work with all thy might, and to practice productive enterprise.

In terms of things that people need and want and which they will happily pay money for, what comes to your mind?

Clothing is one such item. If you can produce high-quality cotton clothing at a reasonable price, something no one in the world is doing right now, you will be in position to make a lot of money.

How about air conditioning? People need it and want it. If you could produce an inexpensive portable air conditioner, you could make millions of dollars and have fun doing so.

Let your mind do a little thinking. Ask yourself what people need and want, and then combine your answers with your own particular skills and talents. Million-dollar ideas are all around you.

Now that you know the three principals of money, the next question becomes how much money should you make? How rich should you become? For answers to those questions, simply turn to the next chapter.

Chapter Three

Should YOU Become Rich?

It's hard to be holy when you can't pay the rent. It's hard to be a saint when you can't afford food and are forced to subsist on mayonnaise sandwiches; when you don't have a roof over your head and are living alone on the streets with nothing more than the clothes on your back. I know. I've been there.

When I was sixteen, my parents kicked me out and I spent six months living outside and sleeping in parks, on beaches, and under trucks and carnival rides. I had thirty cents in my pocket and everything I owned fit inside a paper bag. The clothes I wore were lifted from Goodwill bins. A milkshake at McDonald's was often my only meal for the day. It's hard to be holy under those circumstances.

It's hard to be holy when one is working two or three jobs and up to fourteen hours a day, just to get by. Or when one has no job at all. People lose faith when they're struggling financially. When a person is subjected to extreme poverty, their thoughts and actions are focused on pure survival, and pure survival tends to bring out a person's baser instincts.

At the same time, it's hard to be holy when you're rolling in money. Money provides time and easy access to a whole host of sins. I've been there too.

When one has money, they become preoccupied with two basic thoughts: how to enjoy their money and how to increase what they already have. The former dissipates their energy, while the latter occupies their time. Maintaining an estate and keeping tabs on one's investments and income streams is often a full time job. And what good does all that money do? How does it help humanity in even the slightest way?

I've never met a rich person who lifted a finger to help anyone besides themselves. In fact, I doubt that such a person exists. Even more telling, I've never met a rich person that I thought had even a ghost of a chance of going to Heaven. The rich people that I knew who are now dead were all mired in sin. I have no doubt that they are now burning in hell. And the rich people that I know now and are still living are most assuredly on their way to hell.

That's not to say that a rich person can't go to Heaven. Only that I've never met one who appeared to have even the slightest chance of getting there. It's also a reminder of what Jesus told us in the Bible about how hard it is for a rich person to enter Heaven: "It is easier for a camel to go through the eye of a needle, than for a rich man to enter into the kingdom of God." Matthew 19:24

Some will say, "Well, Jesus was exaggerating."

Really?

Exaggeration is a form of lying.

Does Jesus lie? Would He ever tell a lie?

Nowhere in the entire Bible does Jesus make an exaggerated statement, yet everyone seems to think He did it here. They hope to God it's an exaggeration.

Others say that it's impossible for a camel to pass through the eye of a needle. Does that mean it's impossible for a rich person to go to Heaven?

Well, if it's impossible for a camel to pass through the eye of a needle, and if Jesus is comparing such an impossible event to the chances of a rich person going to Heaven, what does that tell you?

By the way, there's another Bible verse where people hope that Jesus is exaggerating and it's even more alarming and more horrifying than what he said about the chances of a rich person going to Heaven: "It were better for him that a millstone were hanged about his neck, and he cast into the sea, than that he should offend one of these little ones." Luke 17:2

Everyone involved with molesting children, with vaccinating children, with bringing children to Pride parades and Drag Queen Story Hours, with turning children into trannies . . . They're all hoping that Jesus was exaggerating when he said those words. The problem for them is Jesus wasn't exaggerating. He was speaking quite literally.

Don't be a wimp about this. Don't be a coward. Remember, Jesus told his disciples to buy a sword. He wasn't

36

kidding. If guns had been around then, he would have told them to buy a gun.

Peter carried a sword. He used it to cut off a man's ear when Jesus was arrested. If he'd swung his sword an inch closer to the guy's head, he would have killed him.

What I'm suggesting you do is far easier than that. I'm not telling you to buy a sword and cut off someone's ear. I'm telling you to not make money the focus of your life and to disengage from anyone you know who is committing sin and on their way to hell.

Ask yourself, "Is what I'm doing pleasing to God? Am I making money in a way that doesn't involve usury, drugs, the entertainment industry, working on Sundays, or anything else that offends God? Am I helping to put money in the pockets of God's enemies, either by working for someone who denies and hates Christ, or by spending money on products or services from someone who denies and hates Christ?"

If you *are* working for someone who hates Christ or buying products or services from someone who hates Christ, you have to stop. You have to stop *now* in order to have any hope of going to Heaven.

Of course, you don't have to take my advice. But if you've read this far, then you're someone who is serious about going to Heaven. And as someone who is serious about going to Heaven, you recognize the truth of what I'm telling you.

Your life isn't your own. It was bought and paid for by the blood of Christ. "Know ye not that your body is the temple of the Holy Ghost which is in you, which ye have of

God, and ye are not your own? For ye are bought with a price: therefore glorify God in your body, and in your spirit, which are God's." 1 Corinthians 6:19-20

If you rebel and say that it *is* your life and you're going to live it the way that you want to, then odds are you won't be going to Heaven. You'll be joining the multitude in hell.

God Never Promised You a Rose Garden

No one ever said going to Heaven was easy. Quite the opposite. Going to Heaven is hard. The Bible tells us that almost no one makes it to Heaven. Saint Vincent Ferrer, who is documented with raising over twenty people from the dead, famously taught that only one out of every 6,600 people who die make it to Heaven. The remaining 6,599 all go to hell.

Do you know 6,600 people?

I don't.

I probably know 5,000 people, at most. That means almost everyone I know and have met in my entire life is either already in hell or on their way there. Out of all those people, maybe one will go to Heaven.

It's the same with you.

Almost everyone you know and have ever met in your life is going to hell. But you don't have to join them.

You can be the one person out of every 6,600 who read this and understand the seriousness of it. The other 6,599 will either dismiss the information entirely, or think to themselves that maybe they'll try it, but then never get around to it.

That doesn't mean they're bad people. It means they're weak, pathetic, and stupid. And what's infinitely sad, what really hurts, is knowing that they are all going to hell.

I compare it to watching people commit painful suicide before your eyes. But what can you do? I write books. I give interviews. I talk to people. But I can't force someone to give up their sins and do what God wants them to do. I can't help someone save their soul if they're hell-bent on not saving it.

Be humble and smart and go to Heaven. Don't be an ignorant fool who goes to hell.

Money or Heaven—You Can't Have Both

In the previous chapter I gave you the key to riches. However, now I'm suggesting that becoming rich might not be the best thing for you.

I want you to be financially comfortable, and if you decide to raise a family then I want you to have the means to do so. But I don't want you to be so heavily focused on money that you lose your eternal salvation.

It would be better for you to remain poor your entire life, yet make it to Heaven, than to be rich your entire life and not make it to Heaven.

As I've said before, I've never met a rich person who I thought had even a ghost of a chance of going to Heaven. Every rich person I've ever met, and I've met quite a few, is either on their way to hell or already there. Conversely, I've known a lot of poor people and based on what I observed of how they lived their lives, I'm convinced that some of them are now in Heaven.

Now you might be thinking that you can become rich in order to use your money to help others. That's a noble attitude, but here's the thing: Other than Benjamin Freedman, a millionaire in the early 20th century and the author of the book *Facts are Facts*, I don't know of a single rich person in all of history that's ever done that.

Everyone who starts out with that goal in mind, who says they're going to make a lot of money and then use their money to help other people, never does it. Before they're even halfway to their goal of becoming a multimillionaire, they've forgotten all about helping others and instead are focused solely on making more and more money.

There are plenty of rich people who *claim* to use their money to help other people, but guess what? They're all liars. If you look at where their money goes and the so-called charities they donate to, you'll see that far from helping other people or making the world a better place, they did just the opposite. Their money lined the pockets of frauds, hucksters, and charlatans, and contributed to making the world a much worse place.

You've likely met people like that. If not, you will. Maybe you'll find yourself working for such a person, or maybe it'll be a friend of yours who strikes it rich. Without exception, they will sell you on the power of money and how they use their money to help this organization or that organization; or how they create jobs; or how their money benefits society. Well, let me fill you in on a little secret: they're all delusional.

The fact is they're greedy. They're obsessed with making more and more money, and they justify their actions by giving away pittances here and there to people or organizations that benefit them. Observe the people in your own life and you'll see that I'm right.

I'll tell you something else. When I was down and out and living on the streets, no rich person lifted a finger to help me. But several poor people did. One guy let me sleep on his couch for three days. He had a family with three kids and no money to his name, but he helped me.

Another guy was my age, sixteen, and he let me sleep at his house for three weeks and then gave me a pair of army boots to wear when I left. His family wasn't well off either. Talk to any homeless person. They'll tell you the same thing: poor people sometimes help them, but rich people never do.

Money is a drug. It affects the mind in ways that most people cannot even imagine. Judas betrayed Jesus for thirty pieces of silver. Other men have killed for a nickel. I personally know four people who have killed others for money, and I know people right now who are literally paving their way to hell through their own greed and avarice.

Have you ever seen a riot? Look at the greed etched across the faces of the rioters. They're looting and on their way to hell, all because they couldn't resist stealing a pair of sneakers, a case of beer, or a bottle of whiskey. In some cases all three. (The one thing they never steal is a pair of work boots.)

You'll see that same look on the faces of businessmen as they plot their next move. You'll see it on the faces of women as they compete for the attention of high status men. You'll see it on the face of anyone who spends their time pursuing money or fame. It's a look of envy and fear.

Saints and the Vow of Poverty

Henry Thoreau said something interesting: "None can be an impartial or wise observer of human life but from the vantage point of what we should call voluntary poverty."

Let's examine that statement, because it contains an abundance of wisdom. When one is experiencing *in*voluntary poverty, it's hard to be holy. *Voluntary* poverty, however, is another story.

Basically, a man cannot serve two masters. You can serve God or you can serve money, which also includes fame, social status, women, etc. But you can't serve both.

That's why so many saints took a vow of poverty. By doing so, it allowed them to devote their life to God without distraction. A lack of money didn't tempt them to sin, because they gave it up voluntarily.

On top of that, it gave them a unique insight into human behavior that they would not have had otherwise. A person who chooses voluntary poverty is able to see both sides—the poor and the affluent—with clarity. People that take a vow of poverty are also practicing the first principle of money. How is that possible, you ask? I'll tell you how.

You recall that the first principle of money is giving before receiving. So picture the Apostles of first century A.D. when they sold their possessions and gave the proceeds to the poor. They gave away what they had and according to the first principle of money they must, therefore, receive something of equal or greater benefit back in return.

What they received back wasn't money, it was something better: merits in Heaven.

If you want to get metaphysical about it, study Emerson's essay on compensation. His thesis is that it's impossible to give without getting; that every action creates an even and opposite reaction. If you give something of value, then something of equal or better value must be given back to you. That's exactly what has happened to all of the saints and religious people who took a vow of poverty.

Whether you decide to pursue that path or not is up to you. It's not necessary to take a vow of poverty in order to save your soul, although doing so will certainly earn you merits in Heaven. However, doing the opposite, pursuing money or fame at all costs, will almost certainly send you straight to hell.

Your Soul, Your Choice

I don't want you to be poor. It was tough for me and I expect it would be tough for anyone who experiences it. And now that you're in possession of the three principles of money, there's no reason why you should ever be poor, unless you choose to live a life of poverty. By the same token, I don't think it's a good idea for you to become rich. There's too much temptation involved with being rich.

As we said earlier, a man cannot serve two masters. You can serve God or you can serve money, but you can't serve both.

Which do you choose?

Chapter Four

A Forgotten Secret to Riches

You've heard the expression, "A penny saved is a penny earned." Well, that's not entirely true. When you consider the taxes and payroll deductions our treasonous government applies to our income, then a penny saved is more accurately worth a penny and a half, or even two pennies. That makes saving money one of the smartest things you can do and one of quickest ways to get rich.

Spending money is easy—anyone can do it. But if you want to build wealth quickly, then every time you earn a dollar—every time that money is fresh in your hands—keep it, don't spend it.

When you commit to saving money and *make it a habit*, your life will instantly change. Doors will open and little miracles will take place. Your money will grow at an amazing rate.

Saving money is going to put you so far ahead of the pack you'll never want to go back.

The first way this habit puts you ahead of everyone else is by giving you a cushion of finance that others don't have.

The reason they don't have it is because almost everyone you're going to meet for the rest of your life spends their money as quickly as they get it, or even before they get it.

They save little money, if any. Then on top of that, they borrow money and end up in debt that takes years to repay. Don't make that same mistake. Save as much money as you can and avoid debt like the plague.

How much of your income should you save? The ideal is 80%. That is, save 80% of what you earn and live off 20%. For adults, that's difficult. For young people living at home, it's easy. If you can't match the ideal saving rate, then just save as much as you can.

The second way that saving money will put you ahead of the herd is that once you begin the habit of saving 80% of your income and living off 20% (or as close to that as you can), opportunities you never imagined will open up and present themselves to you.

Perhaps a business idea that requires capital which you would not have had if you had not been saving money will present itself.

Perhaps your opportunity will take a different form.

When someone has money stashed away, their confidence rises. That comes across in job interviews and could lead you to a position you would not have gotten otherwise. Watch and see.

The more you learn about the world, the easier it becomes to save money. That's because when you see just how corrupt and evil almost every person and every business operating in America actually is, you say to yourself, "I'm not giving those bastards a dime of my money." At least that's the way it's supposed to work. The sad fact is most Americans are clueless about the world and how the money they spend contributes to the moral rot of society. Walk into any mall or shopping center in America and you'll see dozens of low-IQ women spending obscene amounts of money on clothes, makeup, jewelry, and other wasteful items.

Not to be outdone, visit any professional sports arena in the country and you'll see thousands of low-IQ men spending wads of money on tickets, jerseys, beer, and concessions. A lot of these people—the low-IQ women in the shopping malls and the low-IQ men in the sports arenas—are married to each other. Stupid attracts stupid.

If you're a single guy, you're going to find living frugally and saving money to be a terrific litmus test when it comes to women. By making your money-saving intentions clear early on and gauging your potential partner's reaction, you'll have an x-ray screen shot into her mind. Try it and see.

Never spend more than five dollars on a date or outing unless and until you're married. That means no movies, no dinner dates, no nothing. If the girl you're seeing is upset because you refuse to spend more than five dollars when you're with her, then that's exactly the kind of girl you don't want to marry or spend time with. Find someone else.

If you do marry her, she will proceed to spend all of your money, plus all of her own money and bury both of you in a mountain of debt. Then she'll leave you for another man.

On the other hand, if she's cool with you spending less than five dollars when you're with her and she understands your desire to save money, then that is a girl you definitely want to spend more time with.

If she, like you, spends as little of her money as possible while saving the rest, then she just might be the type of girl with whom you could build a life and raise a family together.

What can you do with a girl for five dollars? You can buy her an ice cream cone. You can buy two tickets to the Tilt-a-Whirl ride or the Ferris wheel at your local carnival. That's about it. But that's okay. The best form of "dating" isn't really dating at all. It's simply talking and listening.

Never buy a girl flowers or any other type of expensive gift. It's a waste of money and it will blow up right in your face. In her eyes, you'll be a "soft touch" and any respect she had for you previously will be gone.

Now I mentioned how saving money can act as a great litmus test for women. But guess what? I've just pulled a litmus test on you. If you're upset right now, if you find the advice in this chapter insulting or infuriating in any way, it's a sign that you favor money over spiritual wellbeing. In other words, the information in this chapter is a terrific litmus test for you to perform on yourself!

Have you forgotten everything from the last chapter? Remember, you can't serve two masters. You can't serve both God and money. It's just not possible.

If saving money upsets you, it's a sign to look within and rearrange your priorities. You just might be more interested in serving money than in serving God.

Ditch Your Debt

Debt equals death. Never forget that.

In French, the word "mortgage," which is the name given to the debt a person incurs when they borrow money to buy a house, means an agreement until death.

Pay cash whenever you can and don't get into credit card debt. Don't borrow money from your friends, don't borrow money from your family, don't borrow money from a bank or loan shark, don't borrow money from anyone at any time for any reason.

This is some of the most important advice you'll ever get in your life. Don't take out a car loan, don't take out a business loan, and don't ever, EVER take out a student loan—it's the biggest scam in the world. If some smooth-talking teacher or school counselor tries to talk you into taking out a student loan, run away as fast as you can and never speak to that person again.

That teacher or counselor is likely getting a kickback, and they have no qualms about saddling you with a lifetime of debt in order to collect their commission. Remember what we said about greed and how money affects people's minds? This is a prime example.

By the same token, never lend money to anyone for any reason. Because you won't get it back. That I guarantee you. Sure, the person who is asking you for a loan will swear up and down they'll pay you back. Don't believe it for a second, not even if their intentions are good and they believe they *will* pay you back. I'm telling you with 100% certainty you're not getting your money back.

If someone asks to borrow money, simply shrug, smile, and say, "Sorry." Then walk away. You don't have to explain anything else.

Now if you want to *give* someone money, that's different. I've given money to homeless people and others, but I knew it was a gift. I knew I wasn't going to get the money back.

Never sign an agreement or contract without reading and understanding every word. That includes any agreement that you click on the internet.

Almost every contract you'll ever read—and throughout your life, you'll encounter hundreds of them—contains clauses written in deliberately confusing language that's designed to take advantage of you one way or another.

You have to read and understand every word, and even then I would caution you about signing it. You could sign a contract to buy a car and end up paying thousands of dollars more then you thought you were paying.

The same thing happens when you sign a contract for a smart phone or internet service. In fact, I would advise you to never sign any agreement that hits you with a monthly charge or takes an electronic debit from your bank account on a regular basis.

You have to be careful. Everyone is out to dip their grubby little hands into your pocket and extract a piece of what you worked for. To them it's business. They have no qualms about stealing what you're earned.

If you're a creative artist—someone who writes books, songs, or whatever—don't sign anything that gives away the rights to your work to someone else. I can't tell you how many times I've been approached by shysters, hucksters, and liars calling themselves producers, some of them working for major studios, who attempted to get me to sign away the rights to various screenplays and movie projects I developed.

If you plan on traveling you'll need a credit card if you want to stay at a hotel. Get one with no annual fee and a limit of two thousand dollars or less. Use it only when travelling or when buying something over the internet. If you don't plan on traveling, don't be in a hurry to get a credit card. If you do get a card, pay it off in full immediately every month.

Don't confuse living frugally or being thrifty with being a miser. A thrifty person is one who makes the most out of what they have. They enjoy saving money and they make a game out of it. They tend to be happy people, and are willing to share what they know and what they have with others.

Misers are the exact opposite.

The word "miser" comes from the word "miserable." Misers are miserable people who create misery for everyone around them. They take, but never give.

Misers haggle over prices and browbeat shop owners into selling their merchandise as cheaply as possible. They're swindlers who take advantage of any opportunity to steal another person's money or property or to cheat them out of something that is rightfully theirs.

Misers are horrible, disgusting people who are never satisfied with what they have. They pay their employees as little as possible—minimum wage if they can get away with it—and they almost never give their employees raises.

Surprisingly, or maybe not, most misers are extremely rich. They're multi-millionaires and multi-billionaires. The people who run the world today are all multi-billionaires and they are all misers. They're not satisfied with what they already have—they want to take what's yours too. They want everything and they're very happy to start wars, create famines, and force vaccinate people with poison in order to do that.

They enjoy watching other people starve to death while they consume sumptuous meals of steak, lobster, and caviar. At this moment, they're pushing the world to give up meat and eat bugs instead. (For the record, if some fat, pink-haired Communist professor tries to talk you into eating bugs, tell her what she can do with them.)

The mindset of a miser is rooted in scarcity—the belief that there's not enough to go around for everyone. That's why misers want to keep everything for themselves and leave nothing for anybody else. Unlike thrifty people who are willing to share what they have, misers refuse to share anything. Misers are selfish and mentally ill.

Before we end this chapter, here are some quick money-saving tips:

Outside of a broken bone or a gunshot wound, avoid all doctors. They're quacks and charlatans. Don't give them a penny.

Don't pay for cable television or streaming services. You shouldn't be watching television anyway.

Don't pay for insurance, it's a scam and a fraud.

Don't join a gym. You can build a marvelous body without weights and machines.

Don't get your hair cut so often. It looks good long and you'll save money.

Take advantage of your local library and read books for free.

If you make a game out of saving money, it can be a lot of fun. And once your savings start to grow, it becomes even more fun. Just remember to keep your life in balance.

Your Soul, Your Choice

You now have all of the information you need to make as much money as you possibly want. However, as I told you earlier, I consider spiritual wealth the only wealth worth pursuing. Money won't help you go to Heaven or keep you from going to hell. In fact, money can be a great hindrance when it comes to going to Heaven. I don't want that to happen to you. I want to see you in Heaven. With that in mind, we'll dive deeper into the secrets of spiritual wealth in the next two chapters.

Chapter Five

God Wants You Here

Now that you're rolling in dough and making tons of money, what's your next move? If you're happy with the things of this world, just keep on doing what you're doing. Keep making more and more money. That's the American Dream, isn't it? That's what almost everyone on earth aspires to, don't they? Success! Money! Yippee! Then they die and go to hell. And it's true for almost everyone. Very few people are saved. Very few people make it to Heaven.

If you want to be one of those precious few, if you want to go to Heaven yourself, then in addition to making money in ways that are pleasing to God, there are other things you must do. Things that almost nobody on earth is aware of and whose mere mention sends people of bad will into foaming, spitting, uncontrollable rage. We'll cover one of those requirements in this chapter. Odds are you won't like it. But as we noted before, nobody ever said going to Heaven was easy. It's not. It's reserved for the strongest of the strong.

In the book *How to Go to Heaven: Your Proven Step-by-Step Plan to Achieve Eternal Salvation*, I went into great detail about the most important necessity for anyone who wants to go to Heaven. Here's what it boils down to: every person that we know with a high degree of certainty is now in Heaven, and that includes all of the Apostles except Judas, all of the martyrs, all of the saints, Padre Pio (the holiest man of the 20th century), the three seers of Fatima, all them— belonged to the traditional Catholic Church. At the same time, we have zero evidence that anyone who died outside of the Catholic Church is now in Heaven. That's a pretty startling difference. Yet it's all confirmed by the Bible.

All of the teachings of the Catholic Church, from the appointment of Peter as the first pope of the Catholic Church (Matthew 16:18-19), to confessing one's sins to a validly ordained priest (John 20:23) is verified in the Bible, including the Hail Mary prayer (Luke 1:28 and 1:42) and the Immaculate Heart of Mary (Luke 2:35).

You can prove this to yourself quite easily by picking up a Bible and reading it. (For some reason, those who are most opposed to the Catholic Church never seem to want to read the Bible.) You can also read the book *The Bible Proves the Teaching of the Catholic Church* by Brother Peter Dimond which contains 124 pages of detailed information on this subject.

If you don't already know that everything the Catholic Church teaches is confirmed by the Bible, then you've been misled. There's no shame in that. We've all been misled. The shame lies in being too proud to admit it.

55

The necessity of holding the Catholic Faith in order to go to Heaven is one of those subjects that people of bad will have a really hard time wrapping their heads around. And almost all of that resistance stems from a lack of knowledge.

There is more confusion, more misinformation, and more downright stupidity regarding the Catholic Church—what it is and what it isn't—than any other issue affecting the world today.

I doubt if more than one person in fifty thousand actually knows what the Catholic Church is. Yet the remaining 49,999 all have an opinion on it. Even among the 1.2 billion people in the world who call themselves Catholic, almost none of them know what the Catholic Church actually is.

So what is the Catholic Church?

Let's start with what it isn't. The Catholic Church is not the clown show currently taking place in the Vatican under antipope Francis.

It's not the series of wicked antipopes that have falsely laid claim to the papacy since the late 1950s.

It's not what's being taught in today's "Catholic" schools, hospitals, and charities.

It's not a pagan religion instituted by Constantine.

It's not a front for the Illuminati.

It's not a front for the Jesuits, whose Black Pope secretly controls the world—a position of such incomprehensible stupidity that it boggles the mind.

It's not any of those things. It's the church that Jesus Christ founded in approximately 33 A.D.

Jesus said in John 14:6, "I am the way, the truth, and the life: no man cometh unto the Father, but by me."

That's an unambiguous statement. It leaves no room for interpretation. In Jesus' own words "no man cometh unto the Father," and by that He means no man enters Heaven, "but by me."

Earlier in the same book of John, 10:16, Jesus says, "And other sheep I have, which are not of this fold: them also I must bring, and they shall hear my voice; and there shall be one fold and one shepherd."

That's another unambiguous statement. Jesus says, "There shall be one fold and one shepherd." In other words, there will be one Church and one leader of that Church.

Then in Matthew 16: 18-19, Jesus says, "And I say also unto thee, That thou art Peter, and upon this rock I will build my church; and the gates of hell shall not prevail against it. And I will give unto thee the keys of the kingdom of heaven: and whatsoever thou shalt bind on earth shall be bound in heaven: and whatsoever thou shalt loose on earth shall be loosed in heaven."

There we have more unambiguous statements by Jesus, establishing His Church and appointing Peter as the first pope. Thus, we can see in language that even a child can understand that the only way to Heaven is through Jesus by way of His Church, and that Jesus' Church was established in 33 A.D., with Peter as the first pope.

Now notice Jesus' use of the word "church," which is singular. He did not say "churches," which is plural. In other words, there is only one church—not two, not two hundred, not two thousand—only one. So put your thinking cap on and reason this one out.

If there is only one true Church of Jesus Christ, and if it was established in approximately 33 A.D., then which church is it? It can't be any Protestant church, because none of them were invented until after the Protestant Revolution in 1520.

Martin Luther, who instigated the Protestant Revolution, was a Catholic until 1520 when he invented his own religion. Before Luther there were no Protestant religions.

The Church of England did not exist until 1534 when King Henry VIII invented it.

The Baptist Church did not exist until 1606 when John Smyth invented it.

And so on down the line.

Every Protestant denomination in existence was invented after the year 1520. Therefore, from a simple process of elimination, we can see that none of them are the true Church of Jesus Christ.

If we take the Bible at its word and accept that Jesus started His one true Church around the year 33 A.D., then the only church it could possibly be is the Catholic Church, because the Catholic Church is the only Christian religion that was in existence at that time. From the founding of Jesus' church in approximately 33 A.D., up until the year 1520, to be a Christian meant to be a Catholic, period. (It still means that, despite the millions of people who claim otherwise.)

Saint Ignatius of Antioch, a disciple of the Apostle John, wrote in his letter to the Smyrnaeans in approximately 100

A.D., "Just as where Jesus Christ is, there is the Catholic Church."

So you can see that the early church fathers recognized the one true Church of Jesus Christ as the Catholic Church right from the beginning.

Remember, there were no Baptists, Methodists, Lutherans, Evangelicals, or anyone else calling themselves Christian until after the year 1520. They simply did not exist. The only Christians on earth were Catholics.

What this means is that anyone who considers themself a Protestant is following a religion made by man.

If you don't believe me, ask any Protestant preacher when his church was founded. If he's honest, he'll tell you. If he's dishonest (most preachers are), he'll lie and say it was founded at the time of Christ in 33 A.D. In which case you can then ask why his particular denomination didn't have any "churches" or "pastors" in existence prior to 1520. Why did they all pop up after the Protestant Revolution in the 1500s?

He'll likely lie again and say something about the "spirit of the church." When you finally pin him down to admitting that his denomination was founded by a man sometime after the year 1520, ask him how he can justify belonging to a church that wasn't founded by Jesus Christ. At that point, your conversation will be terminated.

The situation is the same for anyone who calls themself a non-denominational Christian. Such a person is rootless and following a religion or spiritual path of their own making. They are outside of the true Church of Jesus Christ.

To add more fuel to the fire, consider this: Anyone who believes that the Catholic Church is not the true Church of Jesus Christ must also believe that from the time Jesus founded His church in 33 A.D. and appointed Peter as its first pope, up until the year 1520, there were no Christians anywhere on earth. After all, there were no Baptists, Methodists, Lutherans, Evangelicals, or anyone else calling themselves a non-Catholic Christian until after the year 1520 A.D. So anyone who believes that the Catholic Church is not the true Church of Jesus Christ must also believe that Christianity did not exist for 1,500 years.

And if that's the case, then for 1,500 years everyone who lived and died, including all of the saints and martyrs and all of the early Christians who were fed to the lions, went straight to hell because they were all outside of Jesus' true Church.

Doesn't that seem a little farfetched to you? Do you really think that Jesus would establish His Church and send His disciples out to preach the gospel far and wide, but then wait 1,500 years for His Church to be recognized?

To believe that is a mockery of Jesus' promise to Peter that the gates of hell would not prevail against His church, because to say that it took until 1520 A.D., or later, for Jesus' true Church to be recognized presupposes that hell did prevail— for 1,500 years.

You don't have to be a brain surgeon or a Bible scholar to figure this out. All you have to do is read the Bible. It's all there in plain language. Needless to say, you will encounter an endless number of naysayers who will engage in all manner of mental gymnastics to try and prove that the Bible doesn't say what it actually says. Pay them no mind. Read the book for yourself.

On top of that, don't pay any attention to anyone who talks about "interpreting" the Bible. Or "rationalizing" the Bible. The Bible doesn't need to be interpreted or rationalized. It needs to be read and understood. In fact, attempts to interpret or rationalize the Bible are where all the trouble starts. It's where you end up with fabrications like the Scofield Bible.

Did you know that Bible "interpretation" didn't exist prior to the Protestant Revolution in 1520? That's when non-Catholic translators began "interpreting" and rewriting the Bible, twisting or leaving out the parts they didn't like. Martin Luther was one of the first to rewrite the Bible to his liking.

Did you know that the word "Jew" does not appear in any Bible prior to the 1700s? Nowhere in the Bible does it say that Jesus is a Jew. Or that Joseph and Mary were Jews. Or that Isaac, Abraham, and David were Jews. Those are all "interpretations" added by non-Catholic translators.

Want proof? Locate a Bible from the 1500s prior to the Protestant Revolution and see for yourself. If you don't have time for that, see my book *How to Go to Heaven: Your Proven, Step-by-Step Plan to Achieve Eternal Salvation*, where I provide all the documentation you need.

This is an issue that has damned countless souls to hell; an issue that sends people of bad will into absolute hysterics. It's one of those topics that almost no one has any knowledge of, but that everyone has an opinion on. An opinion put into their mind by someone else.

The false belief that the Catholic Church is not the true Church of Jesus Christ is the primary reason why people avoid it. It's a sad situation because if those same people knew the truth they would readily embrace the Catholic Church. After all, who wouldn't want to align themselves with the true Church of Jesus Christ?

During the reign of Christian Europe prior to 1520 everyone did know the truth and they did embrace the Catholic Church. That's when Europe flourished. The Catholic Church literally built Western Civilization. Today, since abandoning Christianity, Europe is a shambles, with America not far behind.

Further confirmation that the Catholic Church is the true Church of Jesus Christ comes from the many fruits it has borne, through its missions, its art, and its miracles.

Catholic missionaries have evangelized non-Christians all over the earth, saving countless souls from eternal damnation.

No other religion has done that.

The art and architecture of the Catholic Church has uplifted suffering humanity and beautified Europe for centuries.

No other religion has done that.

Most telling of all, the Catholic Church is the recipient of countless miracles that defy the laws of nature, physics, gravity, and even reality itself.

No other religion can say that.

If it's Heaven you seek, don't discount the only religion in the world with a long history of documented miracles. By documented, I mean scientifically investigated by experts, both Catholic and non-Catholic, and proven to be of supernatural origin.

From the Shroud of Turin (the burial cloth of Jesus Christ), to the tilma of Guadalupe (a supernatural imprint of the Mother of Jesus on a rough-fiber cactus cloak), to the Miracle of the Sun (witnessed by over 70,000 people), to the uncorrupt bodies of saints and seers (bodies which refuse to decompose after death), the Catholic Church has it all.

All of the other religions in the world combined do not have a single documented miracle to their name. The Catholic Church has thousands.

Let's look briefly at one aspect of the miracles associated with the Catholic Church—resurrecting the dead. Starting with Jesus Christ Himself, members of the Catholic Church, and *only* members of the Catholic Church, have raised the dead. Saint Peter and Saint Paul both raised people from the dead. So did Saint Benedict, Saint Anthony, Saint Bernard, Saint John Bosco, Saint Hilary, and many other Catholic saints.

Saint Vincent Ferrer raised over twenty people from the dead, and Saint Patrick, for whom the holiday is named, raised over thirty people from the dead.

All of those cases of resurrection were investigated by both Catholic and non-Catholic sources. All of them were deemed authentic miracles. Meanwhile, with thousands of years to do so, no member of a non-Catholic religion has ever raised a single person from the dead; certainly no Protestant preacher has ever done it. Isn't it time you joined the winning side?

If it's God's love you desire, consider carefully a religion whose churches, hospitals, schools, and missions have done more good for more people than any other organization in the history of the world.

Don't be in a rush to dismiss a religion that has saved Christianity and Western Civilization from destruction many times over. If not for the Catholic Church, the entire world today would be speaking Arabic and practicing Islam. In fact, you would likely have never been born if it wasn't for the heroic bravery of the Catholic Church.

As recently as 1683, militant Moslems were at the gates of Vienna, threatening to overrun all of Europe and on the verge of victory, before they were repelled by the Polish King Jan Sobieski, who led the most epic cavalry charge in all of history—20,000 Catholic horsemen against 143,000 Islamic invaders. Had Sobieski failed, all of Europe would have fallen. The triumphant king and his men credited their victory to attendance at Catholic Mass that morning.

For centuries, the Catholic Church has been the only power on earth strong enough to stand up to the evils of Communism and it remains so today.

Without the Catholic Church the entire world would fall into a dark abyss and we're seeing that take place before our very eyes as one nation after another abandons Christianity and falls into darkness. Europe has fallen. Australia and New Zealand have fallen. Mexico has fallen. Canada has fallen.

The United States has fallen. The world is on the brink of a total eclipse.

Finally, don't forget that the Catholic Church gave us the Bible. Without the tireless efforts put forth by dedicated Catholic monks over the centuries, copying the Bible manuscripts by hand, the entire New Testament would not exist.

A Final Step on the Road to Heaven

Now that we've established what the Catholic Church is—the true Church of Jesus Christ—there's another piece of the puzzle we have to look at. It's an issue of immense importance and one whose mere mention is enough to send people of bad will into spastic rage. That's because even among those who know that holding the Catholic Faith is necessary for salvation, there exists immense confusion over what that Faith actually is.

The confusion stems from the Vatican II Council that took place in the 1960s when an entirely new religion was created. Just as Martin Luther invented his own religion in 1520, antipope Paul VI invented a new religion in the 1960s. Even worse, Paul VI called his new religion Catholic and convinced countless followers that it was an improvement over the traditional Catholic Church. Since then, billions of people have been duped into believing that the new religion Paul VI invented is the actual Catholic Church. Nothing could be further from the truth.

It's a frightening subject and reminiscent of the famous quote by former FBI director J. Edgar Hoover: "The individual is handicapped by coming face-to-face with a conspiracy so monstrous he cannot believe it exists. The American mind simply has not come to a realization of the evil which has been introduced into our midst. It rejects even the assumption that human creatures could espouse a philosophy which must ultimately destroy all that is good and decent."

Since Hoover uttered those words in August of 1956, the situation has only gotten worse. In 1956, the enemy lay concealed, like a snake in the grass, quietly plotting and carrying out its objectives. It was very hard then for the average person to spot the Communist subversion and takeover of the country that was taking place.

Today nothing is concealed. The enemy is blatantly out in the open and the fruits of Paul VI's new religion are there for everyone to see. So let's examine the situation. And as we have done throughout this book, let us do it with a preponderance of facts and evidence toward which nobody can offer a shred of rebuttal in any form. Fasten your seat belt and hold on tight. People of bad will are going to have their heads exploding all over the next chapter.

Your Soul, Your Choice

God wants you in the Catholic Church—the *real* Catholic Church. You won't go to Heaven without it. Now that you understand that, it's a simple process of converting to the True Faith. But before we cover the steps to convert, it's in your best interest to read the next chapter so you can be sure that you are converting to the *real* Catholic Church and not to the counterfeit church invented by Paul VI.

"There is indeed one universal Church of the faithful, outside of which nobody is saved."—Pope Innocent III, *Fourth Lateran Council*

Chapter Six

God *Doesn't* Want You Here

We saw in the last chapter that one reason why people avoid the Catholic Church is due to the false belief that it is not the true Church of Jesus Christ. No one has ever told them the truth that the Catholic Church *is* the true Church of Jesus Christ, established in 33 A.D., and that God has reserved salvation only for those who are baptized by water in the Catholic Church. As a result, billions of souls are now in hell and billions more are following in their footsteps.

Even worse, billions of other souls are now in hell, with billions more right behind them, because they are following a facsimile of the Catholic Church and not the real thing. They are either unaware or unwilling to admit that a counterfeit church has usurped both the Vatican and the Church's physical structures and has been impersonating the Catholic Church since the 1960s.

Have you ever seen a counterfeit twenty dollar bill? At first glance, the bill looks real. It's only upon closer inspection that you notice the subtle differences; the telltale signs that what you hold in your hand is phony and not the real thing. Once spotted, however, the fakery appears so obvious that you wonder how you were ever fooled to begin with. That is the situation today with the Catholic Church.

What people around the world today believe to be the Catholic Church is not the Catholic Church at all. It is a counterfeit church; a new religion invented by Paul VI that is not Catholic but pagan to its core, and one that is leading billions of souls to hell.

Just like a phony twenty dollar bill, the counterfeit church appears real. Its members occupy the same buildings and physical structures. They wear the same vestments and recite prayers that closely resemble the old ones.

To someone not paying attention everything looks and sounds exactly the same. It's only upon closer inspection that the deception becomes obvious and, once spotted, cannot be denied. The Catholic Church has been infiltrated and subverted from within.

That doesn't mean the Catholic Church is vanquished. Jesus promised that would never happen when He appointed Peter the first pope and said, "And I say also unto thee, That thou art Peter, and upon this rock I will build my church; and the gates of hell shall not prevail against it." (Matthew 16:18)

The Catholic Church remains alive today, but only through the efforts of a small handful of faithful followers. It does not exist in any of the churches, schools, hospitals, charities, or other organizations that call themselves

Catholic; or in Rome which has become, as Our Lady of La Salette predicted, "The seat of the Antichrist."

When the average person, who doesn't have a clue what's going on, hears about the infiltration and subversion of the Church, they immediately deny it by citing those words of Jesus: "and the gates of hell shall not prevail against it."

What they fail to understand is that the Communist infiltration and subversion of the Church doesn't mean the real Church no longer exists. The subversion and takeover of the Church's physical structures and the survival of the true Catholic Church is not an "either-or" proposition. Both can exist simultaneously. And that is exactly what we have.

The Catholic Church still exists and always will, just as Jesus promised it would. But it's not a popularity contest. Its existence is not dependent upon the number of its members.

Theoretically, the Church could be reduced to only one faithful follower and it would still exist. You alone—yes, you—could be the only traditional Catholic left in the world and the Church would still exist.

Here's an analogy to help better explain the situation.

At the time of this writing (May 2024), we have a man calling himself Joe Biden, who is occupying a sound stage in Atlanta that's designed to look like the White House and claiming to be president.

Millions of low-IQ Americans and the entire mainstream media refer to him as the president, only he's not the president and never will be.

That doesn't mean the office of the presidency has ceased to exist. It hasn't. All it means is that an impostor is claiming to be president and a large number of people have been duped into believing it.

The situation in the Catholic Church with current antipope Francis, along with his predecessors going back to John XXIII, is no different. They occupy the Church's physical structures, they wear the church's vestments, and they claim to represent the Catholic Church. Only they don't. They represent a counterfeit church. And just like the man calling himself Joe Biden is not the president and never will be, the man born Jorge Bergoglio and calling himself Pope Francis is not the pope and never will be.

The similarities between the infiltration and subversion of the country and the infiltration and subversion of the Church are remarkable. In the same way that the stolen election of 2020 allowed "Joe Biden" and his handlers to claim the presidency, the implementation of Vatican II in the 1960s has allowed a series of antipopes and their handlers to claim they represent the Catholic Church. In both cases, people who have never studied the issue go along with it, mainly because they don't know any better.

Here's another analogy. Suppose you had a neighbor named John Smith, and suppose you kidnapped him and moved your cousin into John Smith's house. Your cousin could then claim he was John Smith, and he could point to the fact that he's living in John Smith's house and wearing John Smith's clothes to prove his case. If he was clever, he could convince the neighbors and legal authorities that he was John Smith. But none of those things would make him John Smith. He would forever be an impostor.

That's the situation with the Catholic Church today. Usurpers have taken over the Church's buildings and physical structures, they've donned the Church's clothes and vestments, they've done their best to convince over a billion naïve followers that they actually are the Catholic Church, only they are NOT the Catholic Church and never will be.

Once you understand that, everything else becomes crystal clear. And you quickly recognize another reason why so many people today reject the Catholic Church. They do so because they believe the Catholic Church is a cesspool of sin and debauchery, littered with Communists and child molesters, and professing a false religion. Well, based on what they're seeing, they appear to be right.

What's being presented to the world today as the Catholic Church *is* a cesspool of sin and debauchery, littered with Communists and child molesters, all of them professing a false religion. Only that's not the Catholic Church. It's a counterfeit church. And remember, that doesn't mean the real Catholic Church has vanished or ceased to exist.

The deception we are witnessing runs very deep. Literally billions of souls have gone to hell since 1968, because they remained in the counterfeit church, falsely believing it to be the real Catholic Church.

Today billions of more souls are on the road to hell for the very same reason. No one has told them that what they think is the Catholic Church is actually a counterfeit church, a false religion that is damning souls to hell.

The Communist infiltration and subversion of the Catholic Church was a long time coming. It's a plot that took centuries of planning and culminated with the Second Vatican Council in the 1960s. At that time, the Catholic Mass was changed from the traditional Latin Mass to an invalid and non-Catholic Protestant service, and the Traditional Ordination Rite for priests was also changed, rendering it invalid. Accompanying those changes has been a series of wicked antipopes all falsely claiming to be the pope.

This is the Great Apostasy, as prophesied in the last chapter of the Bible. It was foretold by Our Lady of La Salette when she said, "Rome will lose the faith and become the seat of the Antichrist." It's also the message of the Third Secret of Fatima, which has never been released to the public.

Anyone who gasps and says, "That could never happen," is an idiot. It already has happened. We're living through it.

The Communist Subversion of the Church

How does someone infiltrate an organization as old and as large as the Catholic Church? The answer is simple, and it's the same way you infiltrate any organization, you put your own people inside it.

Manning Johnson was a Communist agent who left the Party and wrote a book about his experiences called *Color, Communism and Common Sense*. In 1953, Johnson testified to the House Committee on Un-American Activities about the massive Communist infiltration of the Church:

"Communists discovered that the destruction of religion could proceed much faster through infiltration of the Church by Communist agents operating within the Church itself. . . .

"In the earliest stages it was determined that with only small forces available it would be necessary to concentrate Communist agents in the seminaries and divinity schools. The practical conclusion, drawn by the Red leaders was that these institutions would make it possible for a small Communist minority to influence the ideology of future clergymen in the paths most conducive to Communist purposes.

"The plan was to make the seminaries the neck of a funnel through which thousands of potential clergymen would issue forth, carrying with them, in varying degrees, an ideology . . . which would aid in neutralizing the anti-Communist character of the Church.

"This policy was successful beyond even Communist expectations. The combination of Communist clergymen, clergymen with a pro-Communist ideology, plus thousands of clergymen who were sold the principle of considering causes as progressive, within 20 years, furnished the Soviet apparatus with a machine which was used as a religious cover for the overall Communist operation ranging from immediate demands to actually furnishing aid in espionage and outright treason."

Manning Johnson was talking about the 1930s and 1940s. That's how far back the subversion goes.

Bella Dodd

Bella Dodd was a 21-year member of the Communist Party USA who used her Communist connections to become the head of the New York State Teachers' Union.

Dodd wrote about her experiences in the book *School of Darkness*. Like Manning Johnson, she also testified before the House Committee on Un-American Activities and spoke of the mass Communist infiltration of teachers' unions throughout New York and the rest of the country.

Dodd was baptized Catholic as a child. After she left the Communist Party, she returned to the Church, confessed her sins, and went on a lecture tour. She is reported to have said at one of her public lectures, "In the 1930s, we put eleven hundred men into the priesthood in order to destroy the Church from within. . . . Right now they are in the highest places, and they are working to bring about change in order that the Catholic Church will no longer be effective against communism."

Dodd repeatedly said that the Catholic Church is the only religion truly feared by the Communist Party, and the only force capable of stopping it. That was almost a hundred years ago. Multiply Bella Dodd and Manning Johnson by dozens of other Communist agents around the world, each of them training scores of men to enter the Catholic Church in order to subvert it from within, add a century of time for them to do their dirty work, and what do you get?

You get a counterfeit church that has abandoned the Holy Sacrifice of the Mass and replaced it with a Protestant service; a church whose "bishops" and "priests" routinely rape and molest children; a church led by a long series of heretical, non-Catholic antipopes dating back to the late 1950s; a church that has completely abandoned Catholic teaching and dogma.

Christian Rakovsky and the Unknown Light

In 1938, at the same time that Bella Dodd, Manning Johnson, and others were training thousands of men to infiltrate and destroy the Catholic Church from within, Christian Rakovsky, a Freemason and one of the founders of Soviet Bolshevism, was arrested and interrogated by the all-seeing Stalinist Secret Police (NKVD).

Rakovsky admitted at his interrogation that the Catholic Church was Communism's #1 enemy and therefore must be destroyed. He then convinced the Soviets to make a pact with Germany for a double invasion of Poland as a pretext for England, France, and the United States to declare war on Germany and thereby further Communism in Europe.

Rakovsky gave his interrogator three reasons to do this:

1) To destroy Germany for printing their own money and prevent their example from spreading to other nations. This is the main reason why they were targeted for destruction.

2) To stamp out Germany's nationalistic spirit and prevent it from spreading to other countries.

3) To weaken and destroy the Catholic Church.

Here are Rakovsky's own words from his tape-recorded interrogation reprinted in the book *Red Symphony* by Dr. J. Landowsky:

"Hitler, this uneducated and elementary man, has restored thanks to his natural intuition and even against the technical opinion of Schacht, an economic system of a very dangerous kind . . . he took over for himself the privilege of manufacturing money . . . he has by means of magic, as it were, radically eliminated unemployment among more than seven million technicians and workers.

"Are you capable of imagining what would have come of this system if it had infected a number of other states . . . This is very serious. Much more so than all the external and cruel factors in National Socialism . . . There is only one solution—war.

"We have yet another reason, a religious one. Communism cannot be the victor if it will not have suppressed the still living Christianity. History speaks very clearly about this: the permanent revolution required centuries in order to achieve its first partial victory by means of the creation of the first split in Christendom. Christianity is our only real enemy."

In return for helping to create a pretext for the Allies to attack Germany, Rakovsky, on behalf of his employers, promised the Soviets half of Europe at the conclusion of the war. When his interrogators expressed skepticism, Rakovsky advised them to contact Joseph Davies, the U.S. Ambassador in Moscow at the time to confirm everything he'd just told them. The rest is history.

Germany and Russia both invaded Poland—Germany to rescue its own citizens who were being raped, mutilated, and murdered by Polish terrorists in the Danzig Corridor, and Russia to seize territory—and then England and France ignored Russia and declared war on Germany.

It's worth noting that Rakovsky admitted in his interview that these same enemies of the Catholic Church had a hand in duping Martin Luther and engineering the Protestant Revolution.

It's also worth noting that Rakovsky's interrogation began just after midnight in the early morning hour of January 26, 1938, at the same time that the skies of Europe were illuminated by an unknown light.

Our Lady of Fatima told the young seers twenty years earlier that this unknown light would be a sign from Heaven that God intended to punish the world for its crimes by means of war, hunger, and the persecution of the Church and the Holy Father.

The unknown light that inflamed the skies of Europe was visible on the night of January 25, 1938 from 6:30 to 9:30 p.m. In Moscow time, where Rakovsky's interrogation took place, the time was 9:30 p.m. to 12:30 a.m. As this sign from

Heaven illuminated the skies of Europe, the interrogation of Christian Rakovsky and the plans to start World War II were just getting underway.

The Catholic Gazette

In February of 1936, the London edition of the *Catholic Gazette,* an official Catholic organ, published an article about the Freemasonic infiltration of the Church.

The article contained the minutes of several Freemason meetings in which the plans for the subversion and takeover of the Church were discussed. Here are some quotes:

"We still have a long way to go before we can overthrow our main opponent: the Catholic Church. We must always bear in mind that the Catholic Church is the only institution which has stood, and which will, as long as it remains in existence, stand in our way.

"We have induced some of our children to join the Catholic body, with the explicit intimation that they should work in a still more efficient way for the disintegration of the Catholic Church, by creating scandals within her.

"We can boast of being the creators of the Reformation! We are grateful to Protestants for their loyalty to our wishes, although most of them are, in the sincerity of their faith, unaware of their loyalty to us. We are grateful to them for the wonderful help they are giving us in our fight against the stronghold of Christian Civilization . . .

"Let us therefore encourage in a still more violent way the hatred of the world against the Catholic Church . . . Let us, above all, make it impossible for Christians outside the Catholic Church to be reunited with that Church, or for non-Christians to join the Church, otherwise the greatest obstruction to our domination will be strengthened and all our work undone."

Once again, we see a frank acknowledgement that the Catholic Church is the number one enemy of the forces of evil. We also see confirmation of Rakovsky's claim, that these same enemies of the Church were instrumental in duping Martin Luther and instigating the Protestant Revolution, an event that has condemned literally billions of souls to hell over the last 500 years.

The Church Today

We've just covered four impeccable sources, all from times past, confirming independently of each other a plot to destroy the Catholic Church.

They describe the situation as it was occurring *then*. You don't have to imagine how bad things are *now*. All you have to do is observe what has occurred and what is presently occurring: "Catholic" schools flying the rainbow flag and teaching sex initiation; children being molested and raped in parishes all across the globe; "bishops" embracing sodomy and pushing homosexuality on children; "nuns" coming out as lesbians and feminists, and promoting abortion; antipopes denying the existence of hell, celebrating pagan religions and declaring that followers of false religions can be saved; and it just goes on and on.

None of this represents the Catholic Church. It is the work of the counterfeit church pretending to be Catholic.

The Second Vatican Council 1962 to 1965

The key turning point in the creation of the counterfeit church was Vatican II, whose documents contain over 200 heresies. Here's a baker's dozen of the various heresies contained in those documents.

Sanctification and truth are found outside the Church.

Outside the Church there is remission of sin.

People can be saved outside the Catholic Church.

Christians should promote the morals of other religions.

God is the father of all people.

Interior gifts of the Holy Ghost exist outside the Church.

At Mass, the priest acts in the name of the entire holy people.

The true Sacred Scriptures exist outside the Catholic Church.

Ecumenism promotes justice and truth.

The State cannot forbid non-Catholic religions.

Jesus Christ was the first-born of many brothers.

Catholics respect those with different religious opinions.

Each person is bound by the authority of their own conscience.

Those are only a handful of the heresies professed at Vatican II. There are over 200 more where these came from. As bad as these heretical statements are, they represent only the tip of the iceberg of the damage that resulted from the Second Vatican Council. The worst acts to come were the creation of the New Mass and the changes to the rite of ordination for priests.

The New Mass is Not Catholic

The Catholic Church forbids any changes to the Traditional Latin Mass.

"It shall be unlawful henceforth and forever throughout the Christian world to sing or to read Masses according to any formula other than this Missal published by us. . . . Should any venture to do so, let him understand that he will incur the wrath of Almighty God and of the blessed Apostles Peter and Paul."—Pope Saint Pius V, July 14, 1570, *Quo Primum Tempore*

Despite the gravity of sin involved in changing the Mass, as forewarned by Pope Saint Pius V, it didn't stop Paul VI from perpetuating the greatest crime ever committed outside of the Crucifixion—the replacement of the Traditional Latin Mass with the New Mass.

The New Mass was designed by six Protestant ministers, along with the assistance of "Cardinal" Annibale Bugnini, a Freemason since 1963 and thus an enemy of the Church. Its purpose was to change the Mass from a recreation of Christ's sacrifice to a celebration of man.

To accomplish that, over 700 Catholic orations were stripped, communion rails were abandoned, and communion was instructed to be given by hand to show that the Communion wafer was only ordinary bread and that the priest administering it was no longer a representative of Christ, but an ordinary person. Worst of all, the words of the consecration were changed.

These are the traditional words of the consecration: "For this is my body. For this is the chalice of my blood, of the new and eternal testament: The mystery of faith, which shall be shed for you and for many unto the remission of sins."

Those traditional words of the consecration were changed to this: "For this is my body. For this is the chalice of my blood, of the new and eternal testament. It shall be shed for you and for all so that sins may be forgiven."

As you can see, the words "the mystery of faith" were removed, and the words "which shall be shed for you and for many unto the remission of sins" were changed to "it shall be shed for you and for all so that sins may be forgiven."

Those changes may appear insignificant, but they are actually catastrophic.

The words "the mystery of faith" signify Christ's presence in the Eucharist. Removing them indicates that Jesus is not present in the Eucharist.

Changing the words "which shall be shed for you and for many unto the remission of sins" to "it shall be shed for you and for all so that sins may be forgiven" completely changes the form and intention of the consecration.

Christ did not shed His blood for *all*. He shed His blood for the elect, the members of His Church. Here are His exact words at the Last Supper:

Matthew 26:28: "For this is my blood of the new testament, which is shed for many for the remission of sins."

Mark 14:24: "And he said unto them, This is my blood of the new testament, which is shed for many."

Luke 22:20: "This cup is the new testament in my blood, which is shed for you."

Changing the words of the consecration to imply that Christ shed his blood for all is a deliberate falsification of what Jesus actually said. It implies that Jesus shed his blood for heretics, nonbelievers, unrepentant sinners, members of false religions, even Satanists.

This change in the form and intention of the consecration is not an accident. It was purposely designed that way by the Freemason Bugnini and by the Protestant ministers who were tasked with creating the New Mass. It renders the consecration invalid, as confirmed by no less of an authority than Pope Saint Pius V.

"Now if one were to remove, or change anything in the form of the consecration of the Body and Blood, and in that very change of words the wording would fail to mean the same thing, he would not consecrate the sacrament."—Pope Saint Pius V, *De Defectibus*

"The words 'for you and for many' are used to distinguish the virtue of the Blood of Christ from its fruits: for the Blood of Our Savior is of sufficient value to save all men but its fruits are applied only to a certain number and not to all."—Saint Alphonsus Liguori, *Treatise on the Holy Eucharist*

"According to the Catechism of the Council of Trent the words 'for all' were specifically not used by Our Lord because they would give a false meaning."— Brother Michael Dimond and Brother Peter Dimond, *The Truth about What Really Happened to the Catholic Church after Vatican II*, page 107

What all this means is that the New Mass is invalid. It's not a Catholic Mass. It's a Protestant service pretending to be Catholic. And because the consecration is invalid, Jesus Christ is not present in the Eucharist. You can see that Paul VI didn't just change the Catholic Mass, he obliterated it.

Catholics must not attend the New Mass under penalty of mortal sin.

The New Rite of Ordination is Not Valid

At the same time that the invalid New Mass appeared, so did a change in the ordination rite for priests. Paul VI removed from the Traditional Rite of Ordination every duty administered to a priest that set him apart from a layperson.

The Traditional Rite of Ordination contained this prayer: "Theirs will be the task to change with blessing undefiled, for the service of thy people, bread and wine into the Body and Blood of Thy Son."

That prayer specifically grants to priests the power to consecrate the host and wine. In other words, it contains the essence of what occurs at Mass, which is Christ's presence in the Eucharist. That prayer was removed from the rite of ordination in 1968.

The Traditional Rite of Ordination contained this prayer: "Be pleased, Lord, to consecrate and sanctify these hands by the anointing, and our blessing. That whatsoever they bless may be blessed, and whatsoever they consecrate may be consecrated and sanctified in the name of Our Lord Jesus Christ."

That prayer grants to priests the power to bless and consecrate. It was removed in 1968.

The Traditional Rite of Ordination contained this prayer: "Receive the power to offer sacrifice to God, and to celebrate

Mass, both for the living and the dead, in the name of our Lord."

That prayer grants to priests the power to celebrate Mass. It was removed from the rite of ordination in 1968.

The Traditional Rite of Ordination contained this prayer: "Receive the Holy Ghost. Whose sins you shall forgive, they are forgiven them; and whose sins you shall retain, they are retained."

That prayer grants to priests the power to forgive sins. It uses the same words that Jesus used in John 20: 22-23 when He granted to the Apostles the power to forgive sins through the sacrament of confession. That prayer was removed from the rite of ordination in 1968.

Can you understand the cataclysmic results of these changes to the rite of ordination for priests? It removed their power to bless, to consecrate the host and wine, to celebrate Mass, and to forgive sins. In other words, it removed every grace and power intended for them by Jesus Christ. It made priests no different than lay people and rendered the entire rite of ordination invalid.

Stop and consider the immense ramifications of that. It means that all "Masses" given and all confessions heard by "priests" ordained after 1968 are invalid. It means that billions, possibly trillions, of sins confessed to "priests" ordained after 1968 have not been absolved.

In other words, the person who did the confessing continued to carry their sins, even unto death and judgment. Imagine how many billions of souls are now condemned to hell because they thought they had confessed their sins to a valid priest, but didn't. It's the greatest swindle in the history of the world.

The rite for consecrating bishops was also changed, rendering it invalid. Thus, since the late 1960s, the Traditional Latin Mass has been replaced with an invalid and non-Catholic New Mass; while the ordination rite for priests and the consecration rite for bishops have both been altered, making them each invalid.

If this is all new to you and you are not absolutely breathless by this point, you may want to check your pulse. Everything discussed here is irrefutable proof that Paul VI created a new religion and foisted that new religion onto the faithful under the guise of calling it Catholic.

About Those Wicked Antipopes

It is the teaching of the Church that a heretic cannot be elected pope, nor retain the office of pope, and that anyone who commits the sin of heresy is automatically separated from the Church, whether they are a lay person, a bishop, or a pope.

That is Catholic dogma. To deny it is a mortal sin.

"A pope who is a manifest heretic automatically ceases to be pope and head, just as he ceases automatically to be a Christian and a member of the Church."—Saint Robert Bellarmine, *De Romano Ponitface* II

"In the case in which the pope would become a heretic, he would find himself, by that fact alone and without any other sentence separated from the Church. . . . He could not be a heretic and remain pope, because, since he is outside of the Church, he cannot possess the keys of the Church."—Saint Antonious

"It (the Holy Roman Church) firmly believes, confesses and preaches that no one outside the Catholic Church, not only pagans, but neither Jews nor heretics and schismatics, can become partakers of eternal life, but will go into eternal fire, which is prepared for the devil and his angels (Matthew 25:41), unless before the end they are united to the same life."—Pope Eugene IV, Papal Bull *Cantate Domino*, the Council of Florence, 1441

"Of course, the election of a heretic, schismatic, or female (as Pope) would be null and void."—*Catholic Encyclopedia*, 1914, Volume 11, page 456

"If ever at any time it shall appear that any Bishop, even if he be acting as an Archbishop, Patriarch, or Primate; or any Cardinal of the aforesaid Roman Church, or, as has already been mentioned, any legate or even the Roman Pontiff, prior to his promotion or elevation as Cardinal or Roman Pontiff, has deviated from the Catholic Faith or fallen into some heresy: the promotion or elevation, even if it shall have been uncontested and by the unanimous assent of all the Cardinals, shall be null, void, and worthless."—Pope Paul IV, Papal Bull *Cum ex Apostolatus Officio*, February 15, 1559

"By the heart we believe and by the mouth we confess the one Church, not of heretics, but the Holy Roman, Catholic, and Apostolic Church outside of which we believe that no one is saved."—Pope Innocent III, *Eius exemplo*, December 18, 1208

We can clearly see that the Church declares all heretics to be outside of the Faith and unworthy of Heaven, and that anyone who commits the sin of heresy is automatically separated from the Church. Knowing that, let's take a look at some of the heresies committed by the men who claimed to be pope after Pius XII.

To list all of the heresies committed by these men would require a book 600 pages long. (In fact, someone has written that book, it's called *The Truth about What Really Happened to the Catholic Church after Vatican II* by Brother Michael Dimond and Brother Peter Dimond, and I strongly encourage you to read it.) We'll list only a handful of those heresies here, but enough to convince you that all of these men were notorious heretics and thereby separated from the Church.

John XXIII

John XXIII called the Second Vatican Council and began the formal process of creating a counterfeit church.

John XXIII was a Freemason, and therefore an enemy of the Church, as confirmed by Yves Marsaudon, himself a Freemason and author of the book *Ecumenism Viewed by a Traditional Freemason to Pope John XXIII and Pope Paul VI*.

John XXIII said that non-Christians could be called Christians, because of their "good deeds."

John XXIII referred to Jews as the Chosen People. He removed the phrase "perfidious Jews" from the Good Friday Liturgy in 1960, and composed a special prayer for the Jews which states: "Forgive us our unjustified condemnation of the Jews. Forgive us that by crucifying them we have crucified You for the second time."

John XXIII said non-Catholics are not separate from the Church.

John XXIII blessed the Muslim Shah of Iran.

John XXIII blessed members of false religions.

John XXIII said Christians can vote for Communists.

Paul VI

Paul VI replaced the Traditional Latin Mass with the invalid and non-Catholic New Mass.

Paul VI changed the Traditional Rite of Ordination for priests, rendering it invalid.

Paul VI created a new religion and called it Catholic.

Paul VI spoke repeatedly about holding esteem and respect for non-Catholic religions.

Paul VI called non-Christian religions "noble."

Paul VI praised the Hindu Shinto Temple.

Paul VI recommended birth control.

Paul VI praised the United Nations.

Paul VI frequently wore the same breastplate as the high priest Caiaphas, who ordered Jesus' arrest and crucifixion. It is the same vestment that is worn by High Priests in American Chapters of the Royal Arch of Freemasonry. Wearing it is an act of total apostasy.

John Paul I

John Paul I recommended birth control.

John Paul I praised the intentions of the Freemasons behind the French Revolution.

John Paul I said all the people of the world share the same "father."

John Paul I called Paul VI "a great pope."

John Paul II

John Paul II taught that non-Christian religions, including Wicca (Witchcraft) and Satanism were inspired by the Holy Ghost.

John Paul II repeatedly taught that man is God. The Bible says this is the sign of the antichrist.

John Paul II taught that those outside of the Catholic Church can be saved.

John Paul II taught that all men belong to the Catholic Church.

John Paul II prayed with Lutherans and gave a blessing to Lutherans.

John Paul II referred to Buddha as "Lord Buddha" and bowed before a statue of Buddha in a Buddhist temple.

John Paul II kissed the Koran.

John Paul II organized a World Day of Prayer for Peace attended by the leaders of dozens of false religions.

John Paul II invited Satanists to pray at the Vatican and removed or covered all crucifixes so they would not be seen.

John Paul II prayed with Satanists and participated in voodoo ceremonies.

John Paul II participated in Jewish services, an act of public apostasy.

John Paul II has been photographed numerous times making the 666 Eye of Horus sign, signaling to the world that he is a Freemason and thus an enemy of Jesus Christ and the Church.

Outside of Paul VI, antipope John Paul II is responsible for leading more souls to hell than anyone else who ever lived.

Benedict XVI

Benedict XVI taught that Catholics should not convert non-Catholics.

Benedict XVI attended Jewish services, an act of public apostasy.

Benedict XVI attended Islamic services and prayed in a Mosque.

Benedict XVI claimed that there were "pagan saints."

Benedict XVI claimed the Bible is based on "pagan creation accounts."

Benedict XVI wrote the forward to a book entitled *The Jewish People and Their Sacred Scriptures in the Christian Bible*, in which the author claims that Jesus doesn't have to be seen as the Messiah.

Benedict XVI taught that Catholics should respect false, non-Catholic religions.

Francis

Francis teaches that Jesus will accept practicing homosexuals.

Francis teaches that people in a state of mortal sin may receive Communion.

Francis attended Islamic services, an act of public apostasy.

Francis teaches that all men will be saved.

Francis attended a Buddhist Temple, an act of public apostasy.

Francis teaches that Catholics should pray with non-Catholics.

Francis claimed that Martin Luther was "intelligent" and offered a "remedy for the Church."

Francis said, "Lutherans and Catholics and all Protestants are in agreement on the doctrine of justification."

Any of these heresies or acts of apostasy taken on its own is enough to expel someone from the Church. Yet here we have multiple acts of heresy, one on top of the other, and remember, this is only partial list of the sins these men committed while claiming to be pope.

You can see just from these limited examples that none of these men are even remotely Catholic. They are wolves in sheep's clothing tasked with leading their followers to the depths of hell. Francis is doing the same right now.

Despite such overwhelming evidence that none of these men are valid popes and that all of them have been excommunicated from the Church, countless people calling themselves Catholic refuse to acknowledge that simple truth.

It's an issue that people of bad will have a really hard time wrapping their heads around. All they know is what they see on television and if it's not on the idiot box, then it can't be true. In actuality, all of the heresies committed by these antipopes *have* been on the idiot box, only people of bad will were too busy watching porn to pay attention.

Let's look again at antipope Francis. In addition to the heresies and acts of apostasy already listed, Francis recently toured Europe where he openly and actively promoted the Islamic invasion currently taking place there. It was all over the television news. Yet people of bad will somehow missed it.

In 2017, Francis presented pro-abortion activist Lilianne Ploumen with a medal of honor in the order of Saint Gregory the Great as a personal prize and confirmation of her work in promoting abortion. That was on the news too.

Ploumen is the founder and head of "She Decides," a pro-abortion organization that raised over $300 million in its first year. According to the "She Decides" website, their number one priority is: "Abortion rights for everyone, everywhere."

Just recently, in June of 2023, Francis invited Andres Serrano to a celebration at the Sistine Chapel. Serrano's 1987 photograph entitled *Immersion* features Jesus on a crucifix submerged in urine. When Francis and Serrano met, Francis smiled and gave his friend a thumbs-up, thus signifying his approval for Serrano's "art." That story was widely publicized on every news channel, yet people of bad will didn't care.

Pause and think about these three very public acts of apostasy that Francis engaged in. He openly pushed for the Islamic invasion of Europe and demanded that European countries take in more invaders. He presented a religious medal of honor to a woman whose organization is dedicated to promoting and legalizing abortion, the most despicable crime imaginable. He invited Serrano to a celebration at the

Vatican, and then rather than condemn the man, Francis smiled and flashed him a thumbs-up.

Yet billions of brainwashed people continue to accept Francis and his predecessors as valid popes.

Jesus said, "By their fruits you will know them." The fruits are there for all to see, but the willfully blind refuse to acknowledge them.

You could make the case that none of these antipopes were legitimate popes to begin with, since they all held heretical beliefs before they were elected. In the case of Francis, he was ordained after 1968 in the false rite of ordination and therefore he was never even a valid priest. That makes his entire papal election null and void

There's nothing controversial about any of this. Ask yourself, "Is it Catholic dogma that heretics are automatically separated from the Church and lose their positions of office?"

Yes, you've seen the evidence.

Have all of the men claiming to be pope after Pius XII committed multiple acts of heresy?

Yes, you've seen the examples, and, remember, those are only partial lists.

Have all of these men therefore been excommunicated from the Church and did they all cease being pope?

Absolutely. It is the teaching of the Church. And to deny the teaching of the Church is to commit the mortal sin of heresy.

"After the reception of baptism, if anyone, retaining the name Christian pertinaciously denies or doubts something to be believed from the truth of the divine and Catholic Faith (such a one) is a heretic."— Canon 1325, 1917 *Code of Canon Law*

So there you have it. Case closed. John XXIII, Paul VI, John Paul I, John Paul II, and Benedict XVI are all burning in hell, with Francis soon to follow. Nothing controversial about it at all.

By the way, whenever you hear the word "controversial," it means that someone's power is being threatened. In this case, anyone who calls the excommunication of heretical antipopes "controversial" is doing so because either their power or someone else's power is being threatened. That's all it means, nothing more.

"For men are not bound or able to read hearts, but when they see that someone is a heretic by his external works, they judge him to be a heretic pure and simple, and condemn him as a heretic."—Saint Robert Bellarmine, *De Romano Pontifice*

Your Soul, Your Choice

There's no sitting on the fence with this issue. We have to choose individually whether to embrace the true Catholic Faith or to follow the herd into the fires of hell. Denial is not an option, and ignorance is no longer an excuse. What matters is how you choose to react to this information.

The first thing most people do when they hear these truths is run straight to their parish "priest." But guess what? If that "priest" wasn't ordained before 1968, then he's not a validly ordained priest. He's a layperson posing as a priest. And if he doesn't know the truth himself, how can he possibly render a truthful answer?

Others come across this information and turn to the internet for confirmation. That's all well and good, but the majority of websites that call themselves Catholic aren't Catholic at all. They're Vatican II gatekeepers, designed to keep the clueless within the pen of the counterfeit church.

If you wish to research this topic further, here's where you should go: www.MostHolyFamilyMonastery.com

You should also read the book *The Truth about What Really Happened to the Catholic Church after Vatican II* by Brother Michael Dimond and Brother Peter Dimond. It's over 600 pages of irrefutable proof that what almost everyone today thinks is the Catholic Church is nothing but a wicked counterfeit church.

For those who say God would never allow His Church to exist without a true pope, the Church has had over 42 antipopes in its 2,000 year history. And, as we mentioned earlier, the infiltration and subversion of the Church was prophesied in the Bible. Jesus tells us that "in the holy place" itself there will be "the abomination of desolation" (Matthew 24:15), and a deception so profound that, "if it were possible, they shall deceive the very elect." (Matthew 24:24).

If you're reeling from this information, I can understand. When I first heard it, I was somewhat shocked myself. That is, until I actually researched the information for myself. At that point it became crystal clear.

It might help you to understand how this massive deception was accomplished by studying the history of Communist propaganda. Anthony Malcolm Daniels, known by his pen name Theodore Dalrymple, is an expert on the subject and his words here are especially relevant:

"In my study of Communist societies, I came to the conclusion that the purpose of 'progressive' propaganda is not to persuade or convince, not to inform—but to humiliate; and so the less it corresponds to reality the better. When people are forced to remain silent when they are being told the most obvious lies, or even worse when they are forced to repeat the lies themselves, they lose their sense of probity. To assent to obvious lies is to become evil oneself. One's standing to resist anything is eroded. A society of emasculated liars is easy to control."

The purpose behind Vatican II wasn't only to dismantle and destroy the Church from within, it was also to humiliate and emasculate Catholic men. By accepting a weak, watered-down, non-Catholic religion, those men became weak, watered-down, and non-Catholic themselves.

That has led us to where we are now, which is a classic case of Stockholm syndrome. The hostages (those who remain inside the counterfeit church) have developed a psychological bond with their captors (those keeping them in the counterfeit church), and have turned against those who are trying to rescue them from sin (traditional Catholics).

You're Almost There

This was a long, but necessary chapter and I commend you for sticking it out. If you follow through on the advice in this book, and I strongly urge you to do so, then it is imperative for you to embrace the true Catholic Church and not the mockery of the Faith coming from the counterfeit church.

To become a disciple of Christ and a member of His one true Church, there are four steps to take. First, you must believe in the teachings of the true Catholic Church. Second, you must be baptized Catholic, if you are not already. Third, you must live the remainder of your life as a traditional Catholic. That includes never attending a non-Catholic service like the New Mass ever again, and receiving confession only from a validly ordained Catholic priest. Last but not least, you must recite the Profession of Catholic Faith (included in this chapter).

The first step is easy. You can buy a five dollar copy of the book *The Penny Catechism* and learn the basic teachings of the Church. The book is small and only 70 pages long, so you can read through it very quickly. You can also learn all about the Catholic Church and its teachings by reading articles and watching videos on the website www.MostHolyFamilyMonastery.com and on their companion website www.VaticanCatholic.com.

Once you are onboard with all of the teachings of the Catholic Church, you must be baptized Catholic, if you are not already. That, too, is easy. Contact the websites above and ask if they can refer you to someone in your area to baptize you.

The next step is confession with a validly ordained Catholic priest. That's going to be tricky, because most priests ordained before 1968 are now dead. Still, search your area and you might be able to find one, perhaps in a retirement home.

Don't confess your sins to anyone ordained after 1968, because it won't be valid.

You can also confess to an Eastern Rite priest at an Eastern Rite church, as they have been ordained in the Traditional Rite of Ordination. Look for a Byzantine Catholic Church or Ukrainian Catholic Church. Ask the priest if he has been ordained in the Eastern Rite. If so, then that priest is an option for confession.

Finding a valid priest for confession is going to take some effort on your part. In the meantime, recite a Perfect Act of Contrition. A Perfect Act of Contrition will absolve your sins.

If you have never been baptized before, then after your first baptism, you do not need to go to confession right away as your baptism will absolve all of your sins. Sooner or later though, you will almost certainly have to go to confession.

Once you become a traditional Catholic, you must have nothing to do with the non-Catholic counterfeit church ever again. That includes never attending the non-Catholic and invalid New Mass. Your only option for Mass is the Traditional Latin Mass said by a non-heretical priest ordained in the Traditional Rite of Ordination. As I type these words in May of 2024, there isn't any such Mass being said anywhere in the world that I am aware of.

Since there are no valid options for attending Mass you have no obligation to attend. Attending Mass on Sunday is only an obligation if the Church provides you with a Traditional Latin Mass said by a non-heretical, validly ordained Catholic priest within reasonable distance. Thus, you should stay home on Sunday.

Staying home on Sunday is not as extreme as some people make it out. When the missionaries went out to preach the gospel to the world, they were often alone in the wilderness for months or years at a time. They had nowhere to attend Mass and no one to hear their confession. For the former, they prayed the Rosary on Sunday. For the latter, they relied on the Perfect Act of Contrition. A Perfect Act of Contrition is said out of love for God and our grief for having offended Him.

If you were shipwrecked on an island, God wouldn't hold it against you for not going to Mass on Sunday, because there wouldn't be any Mass for you to attend. The situation today is no different. There are no validly ordained, non-heretical priests offering the Traditional Latin Mass anywhere in the world. Thus, your only option is to stay home.

On the plus side, if you're a non-practicing member of any religion, or if you belong to no religion at all, then converting to the traditional Catholic Church is the easiest thing in the world. There is no Mass for you to attend and that won't be changing anytime soon, if ever.

So all you have to do is follow the teachings of the Church.

What else is required? You will have to detach from the world; to be in the world, but not of the world. You must also pray the Rosary and you must stop sinning.

Above all, you must be persistent. You must maintain the Catholic Faith without compromise while everyone else around you is sinning and damning themselves to hell. It's not an easy task, but certainly one you can accomplish.

If anyone questions your actions, consider the source. If the person you're communicating with claims that the sin of heresy does not automatically separate one from the Church, then they are committing heresy themselves by denying Catholic dogma, which puts them in a state of mortal sin. Therefore, they should not be listened to.

In fact, no one in a state of mortal sin should be listened to. That includes anyone outside of the Catholic Church, as well as anyone who denies the basic teachings of the Church, such as the necessity for water baptism, the dogma that outside the Catholic Church there is no salvation, etc.

No matter how good-intentioned such people may appear to be they have disqualified themselves from any truthful and intelligent conversation. They should not be listened to on any subject.

If you apply such criteria it's going to drastically limit the number of people that you can safely hold a conversation with. But everyone you do talk to is going to be well-informed, well-intentioned, and most likely in a state of grace and on their way to Heaven.

If you confine your conversations to those specific people you can't go wrong. Of course, you may not feel the need to talk to anyone. As long as you're avoiding sin, praying every day, not partaking in the pleasures of the world, and embracing the true Church of Jesus Christ, *you're on your way to Heaven.*

"Whoever wills to be saved, before all things it is necessary that he holds the Catholic faith. Unless a person keeps this faith whole and undefiled, without doubt he shall perish eternally."—Council Fathers, Council of Florence, 1431-1449 A.D.

Act of Contrition

Oh my God, I am heartily sorry for having offended Thee and I detest all my sins, because I dread the loss of Heaven and the pains of hell; but most of all because they offend Thee my God, who are all good and deserving of all my love. I firmly resolve, with the help of Thy grace, to confess my sins, to do penance, and to amend my life. Amen.

Profession of Catholic Faith

I (your name) with firm faith believe and profess each and every article contained in the symbol of faith which the holy Roman Church uses, namely:

I believe in one God, the Father almighty, maker of Heaven and earth, and of all things visible and invisible, and in one Lord Jesus Christ, the only-begotten Son of God, born of the Father before all ages; God from God, Light from light, true God from true God; begotten not made, of one substance (consubstantial) with the Father, through whom all things were made; who for us men and for our salvation came down from Heaven, and was made incarnate by the Holy Ghost of the Virgin Mary, and was made man.

He was crucified also for us under Pontius Pilate, died, and was buried; and He rose again the third day according to the Scriptures and ascended into Heaven; He sits at the right hand of the Father, and He shall come again in glory to judge the living and the dead, and of His kingdom there will be no end.

I believe in the Holy Ghost, the Lord, and giver of Life, who proceeds from the Father and the Son; who equally with the Father and the Son is adored and glorified; who spoke through the profits.

I believe there is one, holy, Catholic and apostolic Church. I confess one baptism for the remission of sins; and I hope for the resurrection of the dead, and the life of the world to come. Amen.

I resolutely accept and embrace the apostolic and ecclesiastical traditions and the other practices and regulations of that same Church.

In like manner I accept Sacred Scripture according to the meaning which has been held by holy Mother Church and which she now holds. It is her prerogative to pass judgment on the true meaning and interpretation of Sacred Scripture. And I will never accept or interpret it in a manner different from the unanimous agreement of the Fathers.

I also acknowledge that there are truly and properly seven sacraments of the New Law, instituted by Jesus Christ our Lord, and that they are necessary for the salvation of the human race, although it is not necessary for each individual to receive them all.

I acknowledge that the seven sacraments are: Baptism, Confirmation, Eucharist, Penance, Extreme Unction, Holy Orders, and Matrimony; and that they confer grace; and that of the seven, Baptism, Confirmation, and Holy Orders cannot be repeated without committing a sacrilege.

I also accept and acknowledge the customary and approved rites of the Catholic Church in the solemn administration of these sacraments.

I embrace and accept each and every article on Original Sin and Justification declared and defined in the most holy Council of Trent.

I likewise profess that in Mass a true, proper, and propitiatory sacrifice is offered to God on behalf of the living and the dead, and that the Body and Blood together with the Soul and Divinity of our Lord Jesus Christ is truly, really and substantially present in the most holy Sacrament of the Eucharist, and that there is a change of the whole substance of the bread into the Body, and of the whole substance of the wine into the Blood; and this change the Catholic Church calls transubstantiation.

I also profess that the whole and entire Christ and a true Sacrament is received under each separate species.

I firmly hold that there is a purgatory, and that the souls detained there are helped by the prayers of the faithful.

I likewise hold that the saints reigning together with Christ should be honored and invoked, that they offer prayers to God on our behalf, and that their relics should be venerated.

I firmly assert that images of Christ, of the Mother of God ever Virgin, and of the other saints should be owned and kept, and that due honor and veneration should be given to them.

I affirm the power of indulgences was left in the keeping of the Church by Christ, and that the use of indulgences is very beneficial to Christians.

I acknowledge the holy, Catholic, and apostolic Roman Church as the mother and teacher of all churches and I unhesitatingly accept and profess all the doctrines (especially those concerning the primacy of the Roman Pontiff and his infallible teaching authority) handed down, defined and explained by the sacred canons and ecumenical Vatican Council I). And at the same time:

I condemn, reject, and anathematize everything that is contrary to those propositions, and all heresies without exception that have been condemned, rejected, and anathematized by the Church.

I (your name) promise, vow and swear that, with God's help, I shall most constantly hold and profess this true Catholic Faith, outside which no one can be saved and which I now freely profess and truly hold. With the help of God, I shall profess it whole and unblemished to my dying breath; and, to the best of my ability, I shall see to it that my subjects or those entrusted to me by virtue of my office hold it, teach it, and preach it. So help me God and His holy Gospel.

Chapter Seven

Separate Yourself from the Pack

If you have read this far and you're still not convinced of the absolute necessity of holding the Catholic Faith in order to go to Heaven—and I would be shocked if anyone *has* read this far and still harbors even the slightest doubt—then I encourage you to research the topic thoroughly on your own.

Leave your emotions out of the picture and look strictly at the evidence. A good place to start is the website www.MostHolyFamilyMonastery.com

Study the Shroud of Turin, the miraculous image of Our Lady of Guadalupe, and the Miracle of the Sun. Read the book *The Bible Proves the Teaching of the Catholic Church* by Brother Peter Dimond.

Most importantly, make up your own mind. Don't be swayed by the whimsical opinions of others who have never studied the issue. Who are you going to believe—Saint Vincent Ferrer, who raised over twenty people from the dead, or some twit with a YouTube channel?

Put your time into research and begin immediately, because you never know when it's your time to go. Look at the millions of young, healthy people who "died suddenly" after taking the fake vaccine.

They trusted what the liars on television told them and they paid for it with their lives. Out of those millions of people who died from the fake vaccine (and continue to die today), I doubt if even one was a traditional Catholics. I can state that confidently, because a traditional Catholic would never take a fake vaccine.

That means almost everyone who took the jab and died is now in hell. Don't make that same mistake by putting off the necessary steps you must take in order to earn your salvation in Heaven.

Parents Are Responsible for Their Children

If you have children, then it's imperative for you to get them baptized and into the traditional Catholic Church. If you fail to do so and they die and go to hell, God is going to hold you responsible. And why shouldn't He? It will be your fault that your children are in hell for all eternity.

Brainwashing Begins Early

While we're on the subject of children, if yours are attending school you need to pull them out immediately and begin homeschooling them. Schools—and I'm talking about every school in the country, including yours—are centers of perversion and indoctrination. And they reserve their strongest perversion and strongest indoctrination for turning children against God.

Every day that you allow your child to attend school is another day of brainwashing designed to bring them closer to hell.

School officials are not your friends. Teachers are not your friends. With rare exceptions, they are the lowest life forms that humanity has to offer. They're salivating at the thought of molesting your children and turning them into trannies. Don't let them do it.

If you're single and looking to get married, don't do it if you're not equipped to homeschool your children. And don't think that you can get married and practice birth control, because doing so is a mortal sin. Either educate yourself and arrange your schedule to the point where you can homeschool your children or don't get married.

Think Differently

If you've learned nothing else from this book, you should be aware of the need to think differently, to think the way that God wants you to think. Because if you don't, if you think and behave the same way that everyone else thinks and behaves, you'll get the same result that they do—an eternity in hell, just like the Bible says.

You might be offended by that, but I would be remiss in my duty if I withheld the truth from you, like everyone else does. That's not who I am.

If all I wanted to do was sell books and make money, I'd write the same insipid slop that everyone else does. I'd tell you to "feel your passion," "believe in yourself," and "follow your dreams." A book like that would sell forty to fifty times more copies than this one will, because that's what people want to hear. They want to "follow their dreams" and be sprinkled with fairy dust. The problem is that everyone who does that ends up in hell.

Did you know that almost every author involved with the self-help, metaphysics field has gone nuts? Did you know that they are all either in hell already or on their way to hell? I can state that unequivocally, because none of those dead authors were traditional Catholics and neither are any of the living ones.

Norman Vincent Peale was a 33rd degree Freemason.

Napoleon Hill claimed he could communicate with demons ("ascended masters"), including the devil himself.

Jack Canfield left his pregnant wife and one-year-old son to live with another woman. His son became a heroin addict.

Marianne Williamson flipped her lid and endorsed rioting, looting, and the stolen election of 2020. In 2024, she said she wants to give the rioters and looters a trillion dollars in reparations.

Jerry Hicks claimed in his writings that he summoned demons through an Ouija board.

Esther Hicks actively channeled demons on a daily basis.

Louise Hay went completely off the rails before she died and heavily promoted both Jerry and Esther Hicks. And it goes on from there. One after another, almost everyone involved with the field of metaphysics on any level, and who happened to push the party line of "believe in yourself" and "follow your dreams," turned out to be someone who could not be trusted. And that goes double for their followers.

Not that there isn't some benefit to self-help teaching, but without the fear of God, which no self-help writer *ever* talks about (because if they did, they'd sell less books), those benefits are useless. The fear of God is where all wisdom begins. "The fear of the Lord is the beginning of wisdom." Proverbs 9:10

Never forget that. Without the fear of God and without the traditional Catholic Faith, all of the self-help teaching and all of the money in the world won't keep you from burning in hell for all eternity.

Prepare for a Lonely Journey

During the height of the phony pandemic, when literally everyone in my entire neighborhood was cowering in fear over a non-existent virus, I put a sign on the inside of my door where I would see it every day just before I went outside. The sign said: Everyone you meet today is mentally deranged.

I needed that sign as a constant reminder of the cesspool of stupidity that I was about to step into. That was four years ago and today nothing has changed. There are less people where I live—many of my neighbors were killed by taking the fake vaccine—and less people are wearing face diapers now (my neighborhood remains 20% masked), but the stupidity is still there. Everyone still believes the "pandemic" was a real thing and no amount of facts, evidence, or proof of its phoniness is going to change their mind.

Here's how Yuri Bezmenov, a former KGB agent and an expert on brainwashing, describes such people: "They are contaminated; they are programmed to think and react to certain stimuli in a certain pattern. You cannot change their mind, even if you expose them to authentic information, even if you prove that white is white and black is black, you still cannot change their basic perception and the logic of behavior. In other words, these people . . . the process of demoralization is complete and irreversible."

Now we're commanded by God to love our neighbor. So I do. I bend over backwards, often at great personal expense, to love and help other people. I suggest you do the same.

However, loving your neighbor does not include being a participant in their mental illness. On the contrary. It means helping to lead them out of darkness and into the light.

As I type these words in May of 2024, there are millions of people around the world salivating with blood lust over the mass murder of Palestinian children being carried out by Israel. Those same people are cheering as police in riot gear brutally beat and arrest college students, not for committing crimes, but for peacefully protesting the murder of those children.

This is the very essence of mental derangement. It's as clear of an example as you're ever going to find of calling evil good, and good evil. "Woe unto them that call evil good, and good evil." Isaiah 5:20

Imagine the level of darkness a person would have to embrace in order to support and defend the mass murder of children. What in their senseless minds are they going to do when they stand before God and He reminds them of his words: "It were better for him that a millstone were hanged about his neck, and he cast into the sea, than that he should offend one of these little ones." Luke 17:2

Do they think that God is going to say, "Well, those were Palestinian kids that were tortured and killed. I don't care about them. We'll let it slide."

What else can they be thinking? They're either delusional to the point where they believe God will forgive them for supporting the mass murder of innocent children, or they're not thinking at all. In the case of the latter, they're merely drifting through life. They're not bothering to think, because they're too busy jerking off to pornography, listening to talk radio, and being lied to by Fox News.

This is serious mental derangement we're talking about and quite possibly demonic possession. After all, who would openly support the mass murder of children other than a person diabolically possessed? Who would support Bolshevik-style police officers beating and arresting innocent college students?

The deliberate mass murder of children in Palestine is something so extreme, so out of the realm of holiness and

116

God, that demonic possession, and the mental derangement that it brings, appears to be the only explanation that makes sense.

It's a level of evil akin to Herod's slaughter of the innocents. "Then Herod, when he saw that he was mocked of the wise men, was exceeding wroth, and sent forth, and slew all the children that were in Bethlehem, and in all the coasts thereof, from two years old and under, according to the time which he had diligently enquired of the wise men." Matthew 2:16

In the same way that Herod was possessed, it's hard to imagine anyone supporting the ongoing genocide in Gaza who isn't also demonically possessed. But while Herod was a lone individual, what we're seeing now is literally millions of people swarming with demonic possession and acting out with energy that spews from the very bowels of hell.

And those who support abortion are exactly the same.

Crisis Reveals Character

What we're seeing now is the greatest litmus test in the history of the world. The virus hoax which took place from 2020 to 2023 was another litmus test. The masks came off and everyone's true character was revealed to the world.

We saw who was willing to fight for their freedom and who wasn't.

We saw the strength and courage of those who stood tall and refused to give in, and we saw the cowardice of those who caved at the first sign of trouble and surrendered without a shot being fired.

We saw those who stood up and boycotted the people, places, companies, and organizations that pushed the hoax the hardest, and we saw the traitors who refused to boycott anyone, who continued to buy products and services from the hoax pushers. It didn't matter to them that the fake vaccine was murdering millions of people. It didn't matter to them at all. The only thing they cared about was their own selfish convenience.

It was a real eye-opening experience, but now the lines of distinction are even more clearly defined. We're seeing who supports the deliberate mass murder of children, and by doing so are complicit in the crime themselves, and who stands firmly against it. You may never get a better chance to see the true character of people as you're seeing now.

It's not a pretty sight.

"To be unwilling to disquiet evildoers is none other than to encourage them. . . . he who fails to oppose a manifest crime is not without a touch of secret complicity." Pope Innocent IV

Your Soul, Your Choice

Almost everyone on earth is going to hell. That includes your friends, your family members, and everyone you've ever met in your life. It's a tough pill to swallow, I admit. But facts are facts.

The Bible teaches it. The Church teaches it. All of the saints for the last 2,000 years have confirmed it. Common sense tells us it is so. But no one wants to believe it. And because no one wants to believe it, they pretend it's not true.

This is the battle you and I are facing. We want to go to Heaven, but we also want everyone else to go to Heaven. Sadly, everyone else doesn't want to go to Heaven.

If you ask them if they want to go to Heaven, they will reply in the affirmative. But their actions tell a different story. In fact, their actions say the exact opposite. They refuse to convert to the true Church of Jesus Christ. They refuse to stop sinning. They refuse to stop providing financial support to God's enemies. They refuse to make their living in ways that are pleasing to God. In short, they refuse to go to Heaven. They are truly deranged people.

You can try to save them. I do. I do it constantly. And yet so few are willing to listen.

The question is where do you stand?

You now know the importance of making money in ways that are pleasing to God, and you now know the necessity of belonging to God's church. The rest is up to you.

"One is where he is before God and nothing more, even if he himself and everyone else thinks otherwise."—Saint Basil

Thank You!

Thank you very much for reading this book. If you enjoyed it, please leave a review so that others will be inspired to read it too. *Your review of this book could be the catalyst that actually saves someone's soul.* Imagine that.

If you would like to join my Intelligence Report email list and receive expert analysis of world events, email me for details.

You can email me here:

mainsmike@yahoo.com

I truly hope you adopt the advice in this book. As I said from the outset: I want to see you in Heaven.

Other books by Mike Mains

The Impostor Sister Lucy

Lucy Santos was one of the three seers of Fatima, where the Miracle of the Sun took place in 1917, and where she was entrusted with the legendary Third Secret of Fatima—a secret so profound it's rumored to have apocalyptic significance.

Lucy later became a nun, but then something strange happened to her around the year 1960. Her appearance changed radically. Most shockingly, she began committing public acts of heresy that were unthinkable and in conflict with her character. Why did that happen? In this explosive new book, you will discover:

- Conclusive proof that Sister Lucy was indeed replaced with an impostor.
- Why the Vatican had to replace Sister Lucy with an impostor.
- Sister Lucy's frank admission that we are living in the end times.
- The true story of the Consecration of Russia—was it really done?
- The explosive contents of the Third Secret, never before revealed.

This is a must-read book for Catholics and for anyone who has ever studied or wondered about the events of Fatima. Pour yourself a cup of hot chocolate and curl up on the couch. You're about to read one the most amazing stories in the history of the world.

The Imposter Sister Lucy: https://amzn.to/2QXq57o

"Very well-written, and it is indisputable that the pictures portray two different women."

"Nourishes the Mind and Soul."

"Fatima is real, but the Sister Lucy presented by the Church after 1957 is not the same woman."

"The author presents all the evidence and persuasively argues that Sister Lucy was replaced by a double in about 1960."

"Real fascinating book—an eye-opener for sure!"

"Every Catholic Needs to Read This Book!"

"This was a great read that everyone in the true church needs to read. It contains facts and truths."

How to Go to Heaven
How to Go to Heaven for Teen Boys
How to Go to Heaven for Teen Girls

Simply put, if you want to go to Heaven, you must read this book. That's literally the best description I can give.

The books *How to Go to Heaven for Teen Boys* and *How to Go to Heaven for Teen Girls* contain the complete text to *How to Go to Heaven*, but with additional chapters on the temptations that young people face, such as drug and alcohol use, pornography, immodest dress, the loss of purity, etc.

God and Your Health

Are you dealing with challenging health issues? Has your doctor told you that your condition is "incurable"? Don't believe it for a second. God in His infinite mercy has provided us with the remedies we need to heal any disease. However, God sometimes sends us an illness as a wakeup call, to get our attention and bring us closer to Him.

If you want to know more about the connection between God and your health, then this is the book for you. Inside you will find information on how to heal any disease under the sun, as well as startling revelations on the relationship between God and a healthy life.

Available in winter 2024.

Monkey Jokes—A Joke Book for Kids!

Tickle your funny bone with these laugh-a-minute jokes for kids. Apes, cheetahs, gorillas, they're all here, ready to entertain you in the world's first and funniest collection of monkey jokes. Are you ready for a gorillian laughs? Then stop monkeying around and get this book today!

World's Funniest Jokes for Kids!

Here they are, the world's funniest jokes and limericks all assembled in one book! Every joke and limerick in this book is personally kid-tested by yours truly! Buy this book today and start laughing tomorrow!

Annihilate Your Acne

Do you suffer from acne? Contrary to popular opinion, acne is caused by food allergies and environmental toxins. Eliminate those causes and acne melts away like a snow cone on a hot summer day.

Bodybuilding for Boys & Young Men

If you want muscles and you want them fast, this is the book for you. It's all here: what exercises to do, how often to do them, what to eat, even how to think. A fast, fun, and effective way to build your body with a 100% success rate.

The North Hollywood Detective Club Series

This mystery book series came about because I couldn't find any books for young readers aged 10-15 that weren't pumped full of anti-Christian, anti-family messaging.

Believe me, I tried. I searched the entirety of Amazon, as well as my local library, only to find that literally every book published for young readers over the last forty-plus years contained some sort of Godless content.

Either the stories centered on witches, werewolves, or demons; or they featured sometimes subtle, sometimes not-so-subtle, anti-Christian content. Every single one.

On top of all that, the writing wasn't so good. It was passable, but almost never beyond that.

Unable to find any appropriate books for young readers that I could recommend to others or give away as gifts, I created my own. The response has been tremendous. If you're looking for clean and exciting mystery and suspense books for young readers, you've just struck gold.

The Case of the Hollywood Art Heist

Jeffrey Jones is a kid with a problem. A *lot* of problems. He's laughed at in school. The neighborhood bully has it out for him. And his parents treat him like a six-year-old. However, Jeffrey does have one ace up his sleeve: He's a master investigator, able to piece together clues and solve impossible crimes.

When the brother of a classmate is arrested for stealing a valuable painting, Jeffrey and his best friend Pablo jump into action and form The North Hollywood Detective Club to investigate the crime. Can two teenage detectives save the day and rescue an innocent man from jail?

"Utterly fantastic!!!!! I absolutely adored this novel. As a 13 year old girl I have found friendship, mystery and enjoyment of this book. It was such a great book that I stayed up until 1:32 am!!!!"

"Magnificent Mystery! I am always looking for that book that will hold me on the edge of my seat all the way through. This author has done that. I have just a handful of mystery authors that I recommend on a regular basis to my students. I now have a new one to recommend when the school year begins."

"Just a short note to let you know that I have assigned your book, 'The North Hollywood Detective Club' as one of the textbooks at our little school, which is located right outside Paris, France."

The Case of the Dead Man's Treasure

When Jeffrey's high school teacher hires him to find the driver responsible for a hit-and-run car accident, he thinks it's an easy case—until it leads to a harrowing encounter with a ruthless criminal and the clues to a hidden treasure. Now he and his friends are in a race against time with a trio of sinister treasure hunters who will stop at nothing to get their hands on the prize. Who will find the treasure first?

"My 12-year-old loved this book. I read it to him at night before bed. Highly recommend it."

"My 13 year-old daughter loves this series."

"Really good book. I recommend it to people who love Sherlock Holmes and detective/mystery books because it is well plotted out. Mains did a great job."

The Case of the Christmas Counterfeiters

While the rest of the world prepares to celebrate Christmas, 15-year-old Jeffrey and his friends stumble upon a plot to flood Los Angeles with billions of dollars in counterfeit currency. Their investigation leads them to a master criminal, his hoodlum son, and a mysterious 15-year-old girl, who holds the key to the entire puzzle.

"The Case of the Christmas Counterfeiters is Mike Mains's masterpiece—easily the best NHDC novel so far."

"My 12yo son loved all three books in this series."

"My 10 year old son has enjoyed all three books. He just finished The Case of the Christmas Counterfeiters and loved it. He says 'It is intriguing and leaves you in suspense. When it seems that there is no hope, something cool happens! I highly recommend this book!' "

The Case of the Deadly Double-Cross

All Jeffrey wanted to do was help a friend from school find her missing father. He had no way of knowing it would lead to his being arrested for the man's murder. Now after a daring escape, he and his best friend Pablo must solve an impossible crime and catch a killer—before the police catch them.

"My 11 yr. old granddaughter loved this book (and the rest of the books in the series). She raved about it so much that her college grad sister decided to read it also."

"My 12 year old son read this book in 3 nights and ended up staying up very late because he couldn't put it down."

The Case of the Jilted Juliet

A mysterious note found in a school library book leads Jeffrey and his friends to suspect that a girl who committed suicide thirty years ago was actually murdered. Their investigation leads them to a quiet sixteen-year-old girl with a secret past, an ex-con with a motive for murder, and a list of suspects that includes their own high school principal.

"Fabulous! Teens and adults alike will love this action-packed mystery."

"Mike Mains has really outdone himself in his latest outing of the North Hollywod Detective Club. Just when you think you've got it all figured out, fresh clues send mystery down a whole new path. Mains brings his characters to three-dimensional life and draws the entire neighborhood in rich detail."

The Great Adventure Book for Boys

Classic adventure tales for boys of all ages: *The Most Dangerous Game*, *Leiningen Versus the Ants*, and *The Hound of the Baskervilles* together for the first time in one volume.

www.ingramcontent.com/pod-product-compliance
Lightning Source LLC
Chambersburg PA
CBHW051834040426
42447CB00006B/525